Sunset

DECORATING WITH
interior
trim

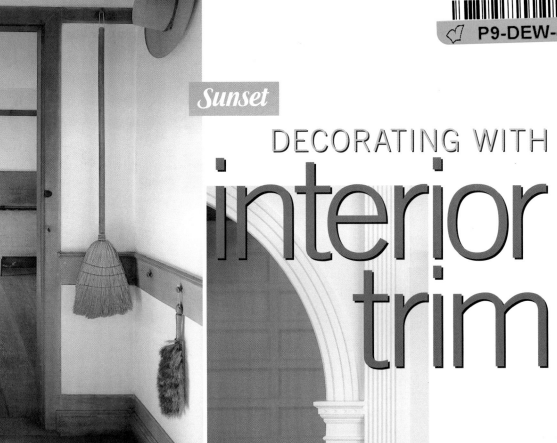

by Lisa Stockwell Kessler,
Scott Fitzgerrell,
and the Editors of Sunset Books

Menlo Park, California

SUNSET BOOKS

VICE PRESIDENT AND GENERAL MANAGER: Richard A. Smeby
VICE PRESIDENT AND EDITORIAL DIRECTOR: Bob Doyle
PRODUCTION DIRECTOR: Lory Day
OPERATIONS DIRECTOR: Rosann Sutherland
RETAIL SALES DEVELOPMENT MANAGER: Linda Barker
EXECUTIVE EDITOR: Bridget Biscotti Bradley
ART DIRECTOR: Vasken Guiragossian

STAFF FOR THIS BOOK:

MANAGING EDITOR: Sally W. Smith
WRITERS: Lisa Stockwell Kessler and Scott Fitzgerrell
PROJECT DESIGNER: Jeff Maib
ART DIRECTOR: Alice Rogers
COPY EDITOR: Barbara Feller-Roth
ILLUSTRATOR: Rik Olson
PRODUCTION ASSSISTANCE: Linda M. Bouchard
PREPRESS COORDINATOR: Danielle Javier
PROOFREADER: Robyn Hessinger
INDEXER: Nanette Cardon
COVER PHOTOGRAPH: Scott Fitzgerrell

10 9 8 7 6 5 4 3 2 1

First printing May 2003
Copyright © 2003
Sunset Publishing Corporation,
Menlo Park, CA 94025.

ISBN: 0-376-01266-8
Library of Congress Control
Number: 2003100378
Printed in the United States.

For additional copies of *Decorating with Interior Trim* or any other Sunset book,
call 1-800-526-5111 or visit us at www.sunsetbooks.com.

CONTENTS

WHEN YOU ADMIRE A HOME, it is often the trim work that creates the eye-catching effect. A classical pediment over a door, deep crown molding, or an intricately carved fireplace surround

transform your home with trim

gives a home character and helps define its style. Trim is one of the most effective tools you can use to give distinction to an ordinary house, or to change the style of a room. And with a little practice, it is one of the easier home improvements to do yourself. ↷ This book is designed to help you select the trim that is most appropriate for your home, whether you're matching period architecture or establishing a style for a tract house. This chapter presents an overview of what trim is and how it's used. The second chapter discusses how best to finish your trim—whether to stain or paint it, whether it should match or contrast with the walls— to complement the rest of your design scheme. ↷ The key to good interior design is to identify and understand the style you want to create, then use it consistently. The third chapter provides a guide to how trim is used in popular architectural styles, with more than fifty pages of trim projects you can do yourself to achieve these styles. Finally, the fourth chapter covers the tools to use and the techniques you need to know to install trim yourself, with instructions on how to make cuts and joints, finish ends, and deal with irregular walls, floors, and ceilings.

why trim?

From the time humans first envisioned home as more than a crude shelter from the elements, trim work has had a place in residential architecture. Ornate stone columns embellished early Greek and Roman villas, carved wood posts and eaves decorated Norwegian farmhouses, and exposed timber framing added detail to medieval Tudor homes. These early examples, however, were part of the building and, as such, not what we mean by trim today, which is additional finishing inside the home—around door and window openings, along walls, and in locations such as around fireplaces. Trim work as a form of residential decoration became popular in the 1500s, as Europe emerged from the Middle Ages. Using patterns derived from the stone masonry of the early Greeks and Romans, craftsmen covered the walls of the grander homes of Europe from floor to ceiling in

plaster trim—built-up baseboards, deep wall panels, ornate chair rails, fancy door surrounds, and heavy crown moldings. Where trees were abundant—mostly in northern Europe and later in America—wood trim became popular, with local craftsmen carving the patterns by hand and with a lathe.

Over the years, the use and complexity of trim have varied, depending on current taste and economic influences. Trim reached its zenith during the Victorian era, when homeowners could buy a wealth of patterns through catalogs—and did, using trim with little restraint. Reacting

in part to this extreme, in the mid-twentieth century modern architects eliminated trim almost completely in favor of pure architectural form. Although vaulted ceilings and open floor plans required little decoration, they did demand high quality in framing materials and workmanship, which were expensive. With the advent of the tract house, cost-conscious home builders began limiting trim to narrow baseboards and flat "clamshell" casings on doors and windows.

In recent years, designers have renewed their interest in trim. Today a wide selection of molding and decorative details is available in hardwoods, softwoods, plaster, and even composite materials such as high-density polyurethane,

Traditional trim— boxed beams on the ceiling, wainscot with plate rail, fireplace surround with elaborate columned overmantle— adds texture and warmth to this personal study, as well as display spaces.

Left Ornate trim typifies the opulent Neoclassical style. Here, dentil detailing on a frieze tops a wide door casing.

Below White-painted beams lower the ceiling in one section of this living room, shaping and defining a seating area that makes the oversized space more manageable.

making it possible to combine traditional styles with modern sensibilities.

Although its most obvious purpose is decorative, trim is also functional: It covers up problem areas, such as gaps where materials or surfaces meet. Some gaps are caused by natural expansion and contraction from temperature or humidity changes. Others are the result of mediocre workmanship. Trim provides a cosmetic fix for either situation.

Trim also protects walls and other surfaces from being scratched or dented. And when you need a place to hang or display things, a picture rail, a plate rail, or even a large corbel does the job with beauty.

trim sets the tone

A well-thought-out combination, or suite, of trim can transform a plain-walled room into a space with style. The effect can range from the cozy charm of a Country cottage to the grandeur of a Neoclassical salon. Trim provides a decorative frame for windows, doors, cabinets, and fireplaces. It can divide a wall or ceiling into sections, giving it greater visual interest. And when a room is large, with unbroken expanses of wall or ceiling, trim can help define and anchor the space, creating a more human scale for living.

In an informal and playful room, a Modern version of Arts and Crafts trim adds interest to the walls and ceiling.

This Victorian room provides a good example of how decorative trim works together with furnishings, fabrics, and colors to define a particular architectural style.

THE BASICS

To employ trim effectively, it's best to follow a few basic precepts.

USE IT CONSISTENTLY Your home will look best if all the trim work conforms to a single architectural style. Formal rooms, such as living rooms, may have more trim—wall paneling, a chair rail, or fancy cornices—than bedrooms, but all the trim should be of a consistent style.

USE IT WITH RESTRAINT Throughout your house, be careful not to go overboard with trim. Too much can overpower a room and detract from all other interior elements, decreasing rather than adding to your home's attractiveness and value.

MAKE SURE ALL THE ELEMENTS OF YOUR TRIM GO TOGETHER Within any style of trim, there are a number of choices. Particularly where trim pieces intersect, your selections need to be suited to one another. For instance, baseboard and chair rail should never be thicker than door and window casings. The vertical pieces on a paneled wall should never be thicker than the horizontal trim they abut. In some cases, such as where a plate rail meets a window casing, the end of the rail needs to be finished with a return (see page 111) so that the end grain is covered.

DEVELOP YOUR CRAFTSMANSHIP Woodworking skills are important when it comes to installing trim. Narrow gaps are almost imperceptible when filled and sanded, but wide gaps and uneven cuts offend the eye. This is especially true with wood that will be stained rather than painted. If you are going to install the trim yourself, experiment with cuts and joints on scrap wood before working with the real thing.

SCALE

The size of your trim and moldings should be in proportion to the size of your rooms. Unfortunately there are no formulas to help you determine what's right for any specific situation. As a rule of thumb, the baseboard and crown molding should be in balance so that one doesn't overpower the other. In rooms with a standard 8-foot-high ceiling, no baseboard or crown should be more than 6 inches tall. Most trim between $3\frac{1}{2}$ and 6 inches in height works well in these rooms.

Higher ceilings demand taller and deeper trim. In rooms where ceilings are extremely high, 6 inches is the minimum height for baseboard and crown molding. If the doors in such a room are standard size, you can make them seem larger by installing wide casings or adding decorative treatments such as a pediment above or pilasters alongside them.

Establishing scale and proportion is a challenge, especially in a unique situation. If you don't trust your own eye to guide you, you might want to hire a designer to specify what you should use and where you should place it before you invest in the material.

Wall frames and pilasters break the wall into sections of harmonious proportions.

trimming it up

after

Developer homes are typically built with nondescript baseboards and door trim, so small, boxy rooms have little character of their own. By adding stained casings around doors and windows and installing crown molding, this homeowner has endowed a plain room with style for a modest investment of money and time.

before

types of trim

The word *trim* refers to almost every applied decorative element you can think of, including baseboard, door and window casings, chair rail, picture rail, crown molding, pediments, pilasters, columns, ceiling medallions, corbels, spandrels, mantels, and fireplace surrounds. Some trim is simply flat boards—1 × 2 battens, for instance. But much of what we think of as trim is *molding,* in which a shape—a profile—is carved into the surface of a flat board. There are literally hundreds of profiles to choose from, although you may find only the most popular ones in stock at your local supplier.

Trim and moldings are generally divided into categories according to where they appear on the wall (although some pieces can serve a dual purpose, such as a baseboard that is used as a door casing). Often different kinds of trim are combined to create a built-up molding, particularly a crown.

BASEBOARD covers the intersection between the floor and wall and protects the bottom of the wall from such things as a wet mop or a vacuum cleaner. The

Wood trim enhances this stair landing from floor to ceiling: baseboard, a window surround, crown molding, and even bead-board wainscot and spindles behind the built-in settee.

A WALL OF TRIM

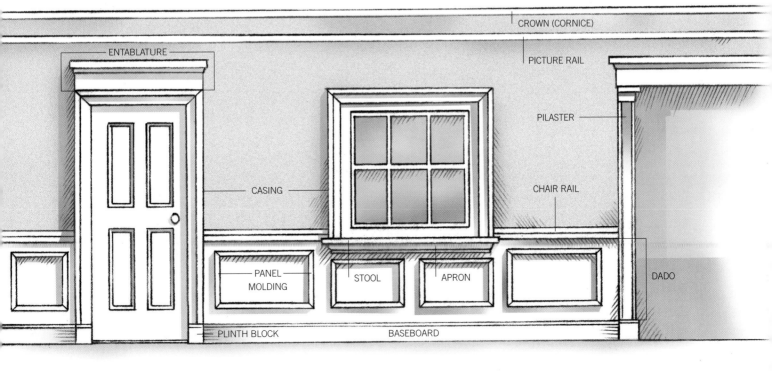

CROWN (CORNICE)

PICTURE RAIL

ENTABLATURE

PILASTER

CASING

CHAIR RAIL

PANEL MOLDING

STOOL

APRON

DADO

PLINTH BLOCK

BASEBOARD

FIREPLACE ELEMENTS

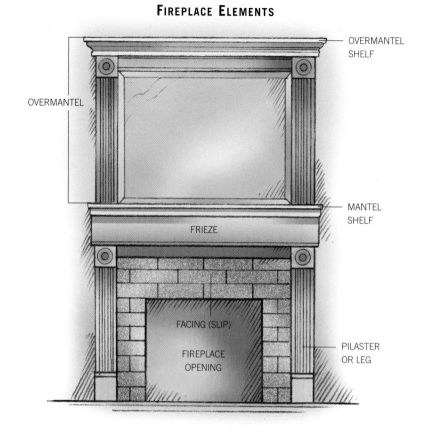

OVERMANTEL SHELF

OVERMANTEL

MANTEL SHELF

FRIEZE

FACING (SLIP)

FIREPLACE OPENING

PILASTER OR LEG

against the ceiling. Crown, which is a sprung molding, crosses the intersection at an angle, so its back is in three parts—a broad, flat central area and angled edge sections.

DOOR AND WINDOW CASINGS create a frame around the door or window opening and hide the gap between the jamb and the adjacent wall. The outside edge of the casings is usually flat, to provide a surface for horizontal trim— such as a chair rail—to butt into cleanly.

WALL PANELING can cover an entire wall or a portion of it. It can be made using frames, panels, bead board, tongue-and-groove boards, or plywood and battens, depending on the style you wish to achieve. Generally, if the paneling doesn't cover the entire wall, it is called wainscot and runs either one third or two thirds of the way up the wall.

CAP MOLDING AND BACK BAND have rabbeted edges that fit over the

profile of the baseboard is generally deeper (wider) at the bottom than at the top. Except in unique situations, baseboard is found in most homes.

BASE SHOE is a quarter-round trim. Its two flat sides form a 90-degree angle that fits against the floor and the baseboard; its third side is rounded. In profile, it looks like a quarter circle. Base shoe elaborates the baseboard

slightly but also serves to cover any gap between the baseboard and flooring material.

CEILING MOLDING (also called cornice or crown) covers the intersection between the wall and ceiling. Flat-backed types are applied at the top of the wall, butting

Built-up moldings, such as this ornate cornice treatment that uses gilded crown and picture molding, are most suitable in rooms with high ceilings.

top of wall paneling or the outside of flat casing.

CHAIR RAIL is applied approximately 36 inches from the floor. It functions to protect walls from the backs of chairs, but it is also used as a division between paint and wallpaper or two different colors of paint, or simply to create a visual break in the wall.

PICTURE MOLDING has a rounded top edge to accommodate hooks. It is positioned high on the wall so artwork can hang from it rather than from picture hooks nailed into the wall.

An entertainment center is attractively hidden inside a built-in Colonial wall cabinet, using trim to incorporate modern technology into a traditional room.

creating your own moldings

If you are an experienced woodworker and own a router, you can create your own profiles out of wood stock. This is especially cost effective when you want a small run of a unique profile, or you want to use a particular wood species that is not available except by special order. Because there are now hundreds of router bits to choose from to make decorative cuts, you can create just about any profile you want. To avoid costly mistakes, practice creating edges on inexpensive stock before you cut into the wood you're going to use.

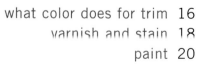

trim and color

ONCE YOU HAVE SELECTED THE APPROPRIATE TRIM for your home, the next step is to determine how to finish it to coordinate with your overall design scheme. Color and finish play a major part in the effectiveness of trim. Do you want the trim to blend into the adjacent walls, or do you want its lines to stand out? Should you emphasize its sculptural aspects or highlight the grain of the wood? The answers to these questions will determine what finish you use. ॐ There are three ways you can finish trim—with clear varnish, stain, or paint. (Alternatively, you can leave wood trim unfinished, although it will be more susceptible to dirt and damage.) If showcasing woodwork is important, you'll want to use either a clear varnish or stain. A clear varnish shows off both the natural color and the grain of wood trim, whereas dark, colored, or white stains change the color without masking the grain. Clear or stained wood is popular in several architectural styles, including Arts and Crafts, Victorian, Modern, Japanese, and Rustic Country. Paint, which can be used with almost any style, provides you with a full palette of colors so you can blend or contrast trim with the wall. Paint can be used over softwood and less expensive finger-jointed wood as well as high-density polyurethane products. ॐ The following pages discuss your options and provide guidelines for helping you select the best finish for your trim. On page 124, you'll find information on how to apply finishes.

what color does for trim

Some trim finishes characterize particular architectural styles. Stained trim is a hallmark of several (see page 15). Brick red, slate blue, or green painted trim, against white walls, is typical of Colonial- and Shaker-style homes. Southwestern-style homes are often marked by vivid hues, such as turquoise or fuchsia, against terra-cotta walls. Pale yellows, blues, and pinks speak of Country style, whereas salmon and gold might be seen in an elegant Neo-classical treatment. For a style-appropriate color scheme, you may want to look through some art history or architectural books for ideas.

The way trim is finished can cause it to visually alter a room's dimensions. A low ceiling can be

Above The soft gray-green of the ceiling beams and paneling gives an authentic look to Colonial-style trim.

Right Faux-marble columns, ornate gilded trim, and pastel walls used here are hallmarks of the Neoclassical style, especially suited to opulent interiors.

made to appear higher by emphasizing the verticality of doors and narrow windows with strong color on the casings. Dark beams on a light-colored ceiling make it seem lower. In large rooms, small doors or windows will seem bigger if the trim is wide and of a different color than the wall. When horizontal trim, such as chair or picture rail, contrasts with the wall color, the room seems wider or shorter than it really is. On the other hand, the room as a whole will seem larger if you paint the walls a light color and "paint out" the trim—use the same hue or a very close variant.

Keep in mind these points of architectural style and overall effect as you decide on the color and finish of your trim.

Bright yellow walls serve as a lively backdrop to cool blue trim, giving a contemporary flair to a traditional room. You can play with different values of color for interesting results (see page 20).

combining trim with wallpaper

In a number of architectural styles, it's common to use wallpaper on all the walls or a portion of them. In such a case, you'll want to coordinate the trim with the paper. The easiest choice is to use a white or neutral paint, which puts the visual focus on the wallpaper. If you want the trim to stand out against a multicolored pattern, paint it the dominant color in the pattern, or a complementary color (see page 20), or use a dark stain. If you want the trim to blend in, match it to one of the lighter colors in the wallpaper pattern. In Victorian and Arts and Crafts homes, styles in which wallpaper was especially popular, wood trim was more often stained than painted.

varnish and stain

It is hard to beat the natural beauty of real wood trim, but staining and/or varnishing it presents certain challenges. First, you should use only high-quality, clear wood trim (see page 100). Make sure it has no defects—they will be glaringly evident on your wall. Then, you'll want to install the trim with perfect joinery, because any defects in your craftsmanship will show through stain or varnish.

For varnished or stained trim, the choice of wood is central.

Each wood species has its own unique color, which shows through varnish or affects how the trim takes a stain. Some woods, such as cherry, mahogany, and redwood, have a reddish hue; others—fir, poplar, pine, and maple—have a more yellow tone. (Most woods change color with prolonged exposure to light; a supplier of fine hardwoods may be able to show you samples of wood in its various stages of aging.) These color characteristics also affect

how the wood appears with other colors, such as wall paint. You can use the color wheel (page 20) to find colors that will look good with the wood you've chosen. Or select almost any earth color for a pleasing, all-natural effect. If you have already chosen your wall color, you can varnish or stain small samples of wood to find the finish that is most complementary.

If you stain the wood, be aware that softwoods absorb stain much faster and sometimes more unevenly than hardwoods. The greater the difference between the color of the stain and that of

the wood, the more obvious any inconsistencies will be. You can ensure more even color by using a wood sealer on the trim before applying the stain.

Stain comes in colors—reds, yellows, blues, and greens—as well as wood tones that can complement any design scheme. If you want a color that is very consistent across both softwood and hardwood trim, you can use a dye stain, which absorbs into the fibrous structure of the wood and changes its color. A pigmented stain, on the other hand, covers only the surface of the wood and gives greater contrast between its light and dark areas. You can control the intensity of color by the amount of pressure you apply to the wiping cloth as well as by the number of coats of stain or dye you apply.

Whether you stain your wood trim or leave it natural, you should protect and preserve it with a final finish. The choices are varnish, polyurethane (sometimes called polyurethane varnish), shellac, or drying oil. (Alternatively, you can use a stain-and-varnish combination product, but the quality of the finish won't be as high.) The traditional finishes—shellac, linseed oil, and tung oil—produce a warm, flat look and can be touched up easily. These are all good choices for unstained Rustic trim. Oil- and water-based varnishes hold up better than shellac. More durable than the varnishes is polyurethane finish, which comes in both water- and oil-based for-

mulations and creates a thick, irreversible coating that is very resistant to water, heat, alcohol, and scratching. A water-based polyurethane is easier to use, faster to dry, and more environmentally friendly than an oil-based one. However, oil-based polyurethane is more durable and will show no brush marks.

Both polyurethane and varnish come in matte and glossy finishes. A glossy finish reflects more light than a matte one—and attracts more attention—so if that's your choice it's especially important to smooth out all rough spots, and putty and sand nail holes before applying the finish.

Above *Stained hardwood walls mute the formality of this dining room.*

Facing page *The Modern varnished fir trim here, influenced by the early-twentieth-century Arts and Crafts movement, stands out against plain painted walls.*

paint

When selecting paint for your trim, it's helpful to know how color works. The color wheel is a universal design tool that aids in understanding the relationships among colors.

USING THE COLOR WHEEL

On the color wheel, the three pure, primary colors—red, yellow, and blue—are placed equidistant from one another around the circle. Between them are the three secondary colors—orange, green, and purple; they result from mixing equal amounts of two of the primary colors. Between the primary and secondary colors are the intermediate colors, each formed by mixing the primary and secondary colors that flank it.

All these colors are full intensity—pure, highly saturated, and undiluted—so they are very strong for home decor. To get milder hues for interiors, you can add either white or black to any color. This changes its value, to paler (a tint) or darker (a shade). A color can also be tempered by the addition of gray, which creates a tone, or a bit of its complement—the hue directly across from it—to form what is called a complement tint.

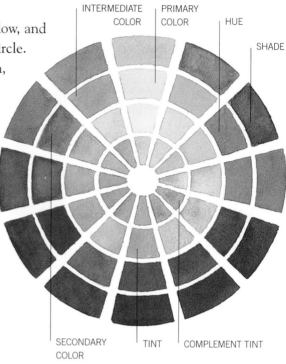

These photos show the same color scheme—green and orange—with very different values. Above, intense marigold walls are balanced by dark green moldings. At right, a soft leaf green tint complements terra-cotta, a dark shade of orange.

ate for homes in Neoclassical, Modern, and Cottage Country styles.

ANALOGOUS COLOR SCHEMES Another way to create a harmonious effect is to combine two or more colors that are adjacent to each other on the wheel, such as jade (blue-green) with blue, or yellow with marigold (yellow-orange). You can mix and match values of adjacent colors for interesting effects. This scheme is well suited to most styles, especially Arts and Crafts, Neoclassical, Modern, and Victorian.

Continues >

Left *A monochromatic, all-white color scheme is restful and reflects the maximum amount of light in a Cottage bathroom.*

Below *This analogous scheme of green and blue is brightened by honey-colored wood, good light, colorful stenciling, and shiny metal plates.*

COLOR SCHEMES

There are a number of tried-and-true methods for combining colors. Here are some of the ones most often used with trim.

MONOCHROMATIC COLOR SCHEMES A monochromatic scheme may be just a single color, or different values of the same color, with the trim either lighter or darker than the walls. If you use just the cool colors—blues, greens, and violets—a monochromatic scheme will make the room seem larger and more open. Using warm colors—reds, yellows, and oranges—can make a large room feel smaller or add energy to an otherwise dark room. Neutral tones, such as off-whites, creams, and grays, create a sense of understated elegance. Monochromatic color schemes are especially appropri-

COMPLEMENTARY COLOR SCHEMES
When you pair colors that are directly opposite each other on the color wheel, you create a dynamic scheme, with each color appearing to gain vibrancy. Here's a helpful guideline when using complementary color schemes: They usually work best if you alter values. For instance, try terra-cotta (orange) trim against a soft slate blue wall, or a rosy pink (red) on a deep forest green. Because complementary color schemes have so much energy, you may find it best to restrict them to active parts of the house, such as the kitchen or playroom. These combinations work well with Southwestern, Folk Country, and Modern styles.

MULTIPLE-COLOR SCHEMES You can combine a number of colors. One successful technique is to choose three that are equidistant from one another on the wheel. A multicolor scheme may take the form of one color on the wall below a chair rail, a second color above the chair rail, and a third on all the trim. Or you might combine colors in a single trim, applying different colors to the curves and grooves of a complex crown molding or the front and sides of a dentil detail. A multi-color scheme is particularly appropriate for high-ceilinged Victorians, where rich reds or browns, blues, and greens are grouped together. In many Southwestern-style homes,

a group of colors such as aqua, peach, and violet adds life to the desert shades of sand and brown. Brighter shades of blue, yellow, and red are common in Modern settings.

WHITES AND NEUTRALS It is always appropriate to use white, off-white, or a neutral tone on trim. Neutral-colored trim is especially effective in unifying a series of rooms that are painted different colors. Note, though, that neutrals actually have some color mixed into their white base; be sure the neutral you choose will match the wall colors you are using.

Finally, remember that one of the wonderful qualities of paint is that it can always be painted over.

This fun and dynamic scheme features strong versions of three intermediate colors: red-violet, blue-violet, and blue-green; the end wall is yellow-green, another intermediate. Save such vivid colors for active rooms, such as kitchens, dining rooms, and playrooms.

You can try out a color scheme—perhaps in just part of a room—and if it's not what you want, select new colors, paint over it, and try again.

DECORATIVE PAINT FINISHES

With paint, you can go a step beyond plain color. Wood or composite trim can be faux-finished to resemble something it is not, adding texture to an otherwise neutral design scheme. Or you can try a finish such as sponging or colorwashing. You can learn from specialty books how to transform simple trim to look like marble, natural stone, or even leather. Start by doing just one section of trim, such as the baseboard, fireplace surround, or casing on an entry door. Faux finishes are very effective in small doses; doing all the trim in a room this way may be too much.

PAINT CHOICE

The final effect of the color you apply to your trim depends on the paint's sheen—whether it has a matte, semigloss, or high-gloss finish. A glossy paint reflects more light than a flat finish and is more eye-catching. This means that imperfections in the wood are highlighted, so it's important to smooth out rough spots and putty and sand all nail holes before you paint. A matte finish is more forgiving.

Trim is commonly finished with semigloss paint to help it stand out from the wall yet not be high-gloss shiny. However, in bathrooms, where wetness is an issue, trim should be painted with a high-gloss finish, which is the most resistant to moisture.

Acrylic (water-based, also known as latex) or alkyd (oil-based) paints are available in all degrees of sheen. Acrylic paint is environmentally friendlier and dries faster than oil-based, and cleanup is easier. Alkyd paint is more durable than acrylic. The higher the enamel (gloss) finish in either type of paint, the more durable it is. For the most even finish, buy the highest-quality paint you can afford and plan to apply two coats.

Applying a decorative finish in the area between stock crown and picture moldings creates the effect of a deeper molding treatment.

using trim to create authentic style

INTERIOR TRIM—door and window casings, baseboard, chair rail, and other decorative wood additions to walls and ceilings—adds distinctive character to a house. Those fortunate enough to have well-thought-out trim work in their home value the way it imparts style and a

finished look. ◌ But most homes built in America over the last sixty years were influenced by the theories of Modernism, which promoted clean lines and minimal decoration. Economy overruled craftsmanship in all but the finest custom homes, so that many have no identifiable style, no personality of their own. Although they may well be adequate houses, we often find them unsatisfying. We want our homes to reflect our own style and character, to offer individuality as well as comfort. Adding interior trim is an effective and relatively easy way to accomplish this. ◌ On the following pages you will find descriptions of the most popular interior styles—Colonial, Neoclassical, Victorian, Arts and Crafts, Modern, Country, and Japanese—and how trim contributes to them, with how-to project plans that will help you re-create these styles in your own home.

In more elegant Colonial homes, exposed ceiling beams were often planed and squared before being painted. You can duplicate this effect by running 4 × 4s across the ceiling, 32 inches on center. Secure the "beams" by nailing them into the ceiling joists.

colonial

The Colonial style, which dates from the late seventeenth century, was not one single look but a collection of many of the regional styles that evolved in the original thirteen colonies.

Although Colonial homes differed in size and floor plan, most were rectangular boxes, from one and a half to three stories, with a gable roof and an entry door placed near the center of the facade. They had one or two main rooms downstairs for family activity, and private rooms on the upper floor or floors. Windows flanked the front entrance; dormer windows were often built into the steep pitch of the roof. The houses were generally constructed of wood because it was readily available and the easiest material to

make weathertight. After the advent of lath and plaster in the early 1700s, the walls and ceiling were covered in plaster, then whitewashed.

The Colonial style is popular today because of its simplicity and the ease of adapting it to the 8-foot ceilings and small rooms of many modern homes. Colonial-style moldings and raised-panel doors, available at most home improvement stores, provide some of the simplest ways to add warmth to a tract home. The most distinctive trim features of this style include the following:

DOORS In the earliest homes, the door surrounds were simple, made from the same structural timbers used to build the house. Later,

four-, six-, or eight-panel doors had molded surrounds with classical motifs. In formal rooms the doors might be topped with a broken pediment that was inspired by pattern books from England.

WINDOWS Double-hung windows replaced casements in the latter part of the Colonial period. A single-piece molded casing was used to frame the windows.

BASEBOARDS A molded 4-inch baseboard encircled the public areas of better homes. Plain board was used in private rooms and in more modest homes.

WALL TREATMENTS Decorative wall paneling graced public areas, with the most elaborate reserved for formal rooms. In many homes, wainscot covered the dado area of the walls, topped with a chair rail; in grand homes, the walls were paneled from floor to ceiling. It was common to paint the paneling, most frequently in earth tones, blues, yellows, and greens.

CORNICES The cornice molding could be quite decorative in living

Left *A stenciled border, its colors coordinated with the bedspread, gives visual emphasis to these window casings. Like the furniture, the trim—casings, chair rail, fireplace surround— is stained dark brown.*

Below *Bold colors and raised panels make simple trim stand out from the wall. The yellowish green used here is typical of the Colonial palette.*

and dining rooms, enhanced by egg-and-dart and dentil detailing.

CEILINGS At first, ceiling beams and joists were left exposed. When the ceiling was plastered, it was most often whitewashed.

FIREPLACE SURROUNDS The fireplace wall provided a decorative focal point. Simple wall paneling that matched the adjacent walls surrounded the fireplace in a modest home. In a grand home, the fireplace might be flanked with pilasters, and the frieze below the mantel shelf carved with classical motifs such as fruit or flowers. The overmantel, often left undecorated, provided a place to hang a painting.

colonial projects

Simple Colonial-style molding will enhance any traditional decor without overwhelming it. Ideal for rooms with 8-foot ceilings, the projects shown here will work in rooms with ceilings of any height; high ceilings can also handle a deeper crown molding (such as the Neoclassical one on page 48). Baseboards and door and window surrounds can be used in all rooms; crown molding, chair rail, and wall panels are most appropriate in formal living areas.

Although it is most harmonious to use the same door casings throughout a house, you can mix casings of similar widths for dramatic effect. Here, a molded casing with mitered corners (like the project opposite) frames a doorway that combines a fluted casing with corner blocks (see a similar project on page 55).

PROJECTS IN THE COLONIAL STYLE

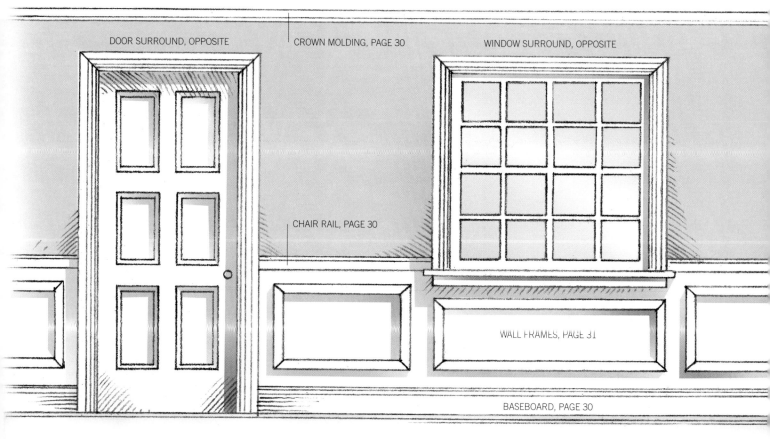

DOOR SURROUND, OPPOSITE

CROWN MOLDING, PAGE 30

WINDOW SURROUND, OPPOSITE

CHAIR RAIL, PAGE 30

WALL FRAMES, PAGE 31

BASEBOARD, PAGE 30

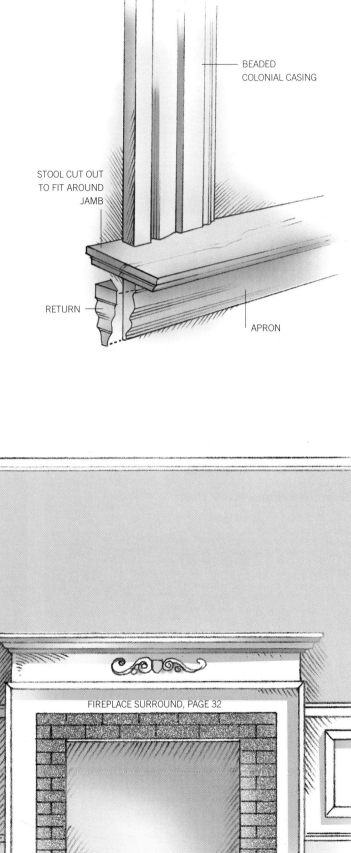

BEADED
COLONIAL CASING

STOOL CUT OUT
TO FIT AROUND
JAMB

RETURN

APRON

Door and Window Surround

See also illustration, opposite

materials

- $^{11}/_{16}$" × $3^7/_{16}$" beaded and molded casing, for surrounds
- $^5/_8$" × $2^1/_4$" molded casing, for window apron

Measure, cut, and install a stool, if necessary (see page 114). Measure, cut, and install the surrounds (see page 112), connecting them with mitered corners (see page 109). Measure and cut the window apron (see page 114), aligning its outside edges with the outside edges of the window casing. Finish the apron ends with mitered returns (see page 111).

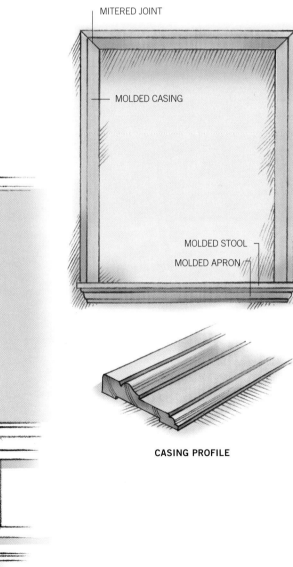

MITERED JOINT

MOLDED CASING

MOLDED STOOL

MOLDED APRON

CASING PROFILE

FIREPLACE SURROUND, PAGE 32

A small shelf gives Colonial style to a mitered door casing. Create this detail by installing carved wood shelf brackets on either side of the door casing and setting a 1 × 4 board over the brackets and casing. A prefabricated split pediment on the top of the corner cabinet in the adjacent room continues the theme.

Baseboard, Chair Rail, and Crown Molding

See also illustration, pages 28–29

materials

- ⅝" × 3⅝" crown molding
- ⅝" × 2⅝" chair rail
- 9/16" × 5¼" baseboard

All horizontal trim should be the same depth as, or thinner than, the door casing, so it can butt into the casing without requiring a special edge detail. Measure, cut, and install these trims (see pages 116 and 117). Connect the trim at outside corners with mitered joints (see page 109) and at inside corners with coped joints (see page 110).

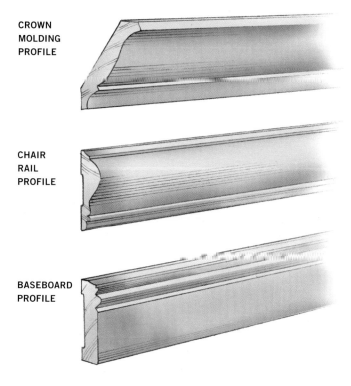

CROWN MOLDING PROFILE

CHAIR RAIL PROFILE

BASEBOARD PROFILE

MITERED
JOINT

PANEL
MOLDING

Wall Frames

See also illustration, pages 28–29, and photos, below and page 50

materials

- $^{11}/_{16}$" × $1^{5}/_{8}$" panel molding

There are several ways to create the look of a paneled wall. This treatment uses panel molding connected with mitered joints. Plan, measure, and build the wall frames (see page 118). To finish the frames, you can paint them the same color as the wall, paint them a contrasting color, or paint the frame and inside panel a different color from the rest of the wall (see page 124 for more information on painting trim).

PANEL MOLDING PROFILE

Common in several architectural styles, including Colonial and Neoclassical, wall frames provide an orderly way to add texture to a wall. Here, a wall frame filled with a subtly patterned wallpaper makes a carefully balanced setting for a painting.

The project below creates a Colonial fireplace surround like the one shown here. If you want a more prominent surround, adapt this project by adding a taller frieze embellished with wall frames and surrounded with other decorative molding (see photo on page 37).

Fireplace Surround

See also illustration, pages 28–29

Although you can purchase a prefabricated fireplace surround —many Colonial styles are available—to install against the wall around a typical fireplace, you can make your own surround and mantel by following these instructions. The following project will integrate well with the horizontal trims shown on page 30. This surround is designed to fit over a flush fireplace facing.

materials

- 1 × 6s, for surround and mantel
- 1 × 2s, to edge surround
- 1 × 8, for frieze
- ¾" × 1½" shingle molding
- 1× boards wide enough to rip to 2½" and 2"
- 1⅛" × 1³⁄₁₆" bed molding

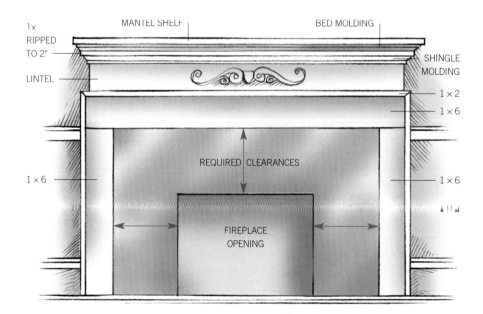

1 Mark Clearance Lines
Decide how much clearance you need to allow between the fireplace opening and the beginning of the wood surround. The Uniform Building Code regulates how close flammable material can be placed to the opening of a standard fireplace. Always check with your local building inspector before constructing a fireplace surround. If you have a prefabricated fireplace, check the manufacturer's specifications for clearance. Snap chalk lines (see page 104) on the sides and top of your existing fireplace facing to mark the clearance.

2 Build Wood Surround
Measure around the fireplace facing. Cut 1 × 6s to build two sides and a header that will cover the existing facing, positioning the inside edges of the boards on the clearance lines you drew. Nail the surround together, butting

the sides into the header. The inside edges can be routed to soften the look and add a decorative detail. Attach the surround to the fireplace facing with mastic, then nail it into the wall framing.

3 Attach 1 × 2 Trim

Measure the distance around the perimeter of the front of the surround. Cut 1 × 2s to fit around the surround, with the narrow edge toward the wall; miter the corners. Glue and nail the trim in place. If you wish, you can rout the edges.

4 Add Frieze

Use the width of the surround without the 1 × 2 trim as the width of the 1 × 8 frieze. Cut the frieze. Place it on edge snugly against the 1 × 2 and nail it into the wall framing.

5 Build Mantel Support

Cut a length of shingle molding, miter the corners, and finish with mitered returns (see page 111); the bottom edge of the molding should be the same length as the frieze. Position the molding so its top edge is flush with the top of the frieze, then nail the molding into the frieze.

Cut two 1-by boards the length of the frieze plus 3½ inches. Rip these boards to 2½ inches wide. Center one on top of the frieze and molding, with its narrow edge tight against the wall. It

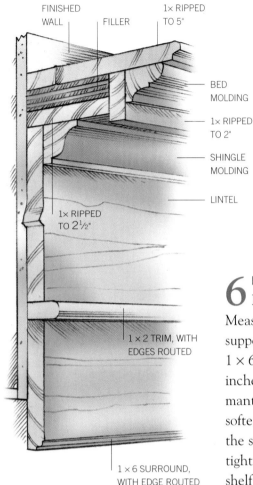

FINISHED WALL · FILLER · 1× RIPPED TO 5"

BED MOLDING

1× RIPPED TO 2"

SHINGLE MOLDING

LINTEL

1× RIPPED TO 2½"

1 × 2 TRIM, WITH EDGES ROUTED

1 × 6 SURROUND, WITH EDGE ROUTED

will project about 1 inch on all sides of the frieze. Nail it into the top of the frieze. The second board will serve as a filler. Nail it into the first board and toenail it into the wall framing.

Rip a 1-by board to 2 inches wide. Measure around the edge of the filler board. Cut and miter the ripped 1-by board to face the support boards. Position the facing boards so their top edges are flush with the top of the filler board. Glue and nail the facing boards in place.

6 Install Mantel Shelf

Rip a 1 × 6 to 5 inches wide. Measure the length of the mantel support boards and cut the ripped 1 × 6 to this length plus 3½ inches. The front and ends of this mantel shelf can be routed for a softer look. Center the shelf on the support boards, with its edge tight against the wall. Nail the shelf into the support boards and toenail it into the wall framing.

7 Apply Molding and Decorative Onlay

Measure the distance around the facing just under the shelf. Cut the bed molding as you would crown molding, mitering the corners (see page 109). Nail the molding around the facing.

For added decoration, you can apply a carved wood onlay to the frieze. Onlays can be purchased at millwork shops or at woodworking or home supply stores. Apply glue to the back of the onlay, center it on the frieze, and tack it in place.

Bookcase Wall

Built-in cabinets commonly lined the walls of formal rooms in Colonial homes. To create this effect, we use unfinished wood bookcases (available through unfinished wood furniture retailers and the Internet), mask them with face frames, and finish them with trim to match the rest of the room. If you prefer, you can make your own bookcases with the help of Sunset's *Basic Woodworking* or *Bookshelves and Cabinets.* You can also add doors to cover the bottom shelves; if your room has wall frames, the cabinet doors can be paneled to match. This project uses one or two 7-foot-high bookcases on either side of a window (the width of the bookcase to be determined by the width of your wall). It assumes a ceiling height of 8 feet.

materials

- 1×8s, for pedestal and bottom face frame
- 1×6s, for top face frame
- $1\times$ boards, for side face frames
- 1×4s, for face frames adjacent to window, joints between bookcases, and side cleats
- 2×4, for ceiling cleat
- $\frac{9}{16}" \times 5\frac{1}{4}"$ baseboard
- $\frac{5}{8}" \times 3\frac{5}{8}"$ crown molding

1 Purchase or Build Bookcases
Measure the width of the wall and purchase or build bookcases to fit. The distance between the end of a case and the adjoining wall should be no more than 6 inches. You may need two or more narrow cases instead of one wide one; the gap will be covered by the face frame.

2 Connect Bookcases
If you are using more than one case on either side of the window or along a solid wall, you will need to connect them. First, clamp a pair of cases together; their top and bottom edges should be aligned. From inside one case, drill holes through one side and partway into the adjoining case, working from top to bottom near the back edge of the side and placing holes about every 12 inches. Repeat from top to bottom near the front edge of the side of the case. Drive screws into the holes.

3 Build Pedestal
So the bookcases will extend almost from floor to ceiling, build a pedestal for the cases. With our 7-foot-high case and 8-foot ceiling, the pedestal should be about 7 inches high (the gap at the top will be covered by the face frame and crown

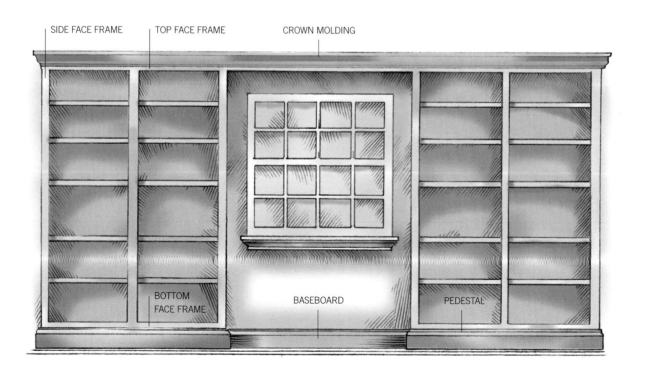

SIDE FACE FRAME TOP FACE FRAME CROWN MOLDING

BOTTOM FACE FRAME BASEBOARD PEDESTAL

Built-in bookcases were an important feature of Colonial architecture, usually, as in this example, divided into closed storage below and display shelves above. If you add doors to your bookcase wall, note that their height should match the height of wainscot or lower wall panels. Built-in furniture is generally painted the same color as the rest of the trim.

molding). The pedestal can be made as one long, rectangular box, its dimensions matching the base of the bookcase, with supports at 2- to 3-foot intervals. Or, if you're combining two or more bookcases, the pedestal can be a series of boxes, each the size of a bookcase unit. Make the pedestal of 1 × 8 material. Don't worry about mitering the corners or hiding the joints, because the face frame will be nailed to the front.

PEDESTAL CHOICES

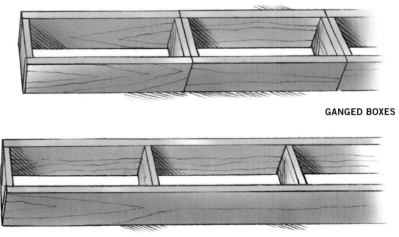

GANGED BOXES

**FULL-LENGTH PEDESTAL
WITH SUPPORTS**

4 Install Pedestal
Position the pedestal and level it, using shims as necessary. Locate the wall studs (see page 108) and screw the back board(s) of the pedestal into each stud along the wall.

5 Install Nailer Strips and Cleats

Purchased bookcases are usually attached to a wall through ¾-inch nailer strips installed on the inside of the bookcase by the manufacturer. If you have made the cases yourself, use 1 × 3 lumber for nailer strips. Nail the strips to the inside of the bookcase—one strip just under the top of the bookcase and another strip just above the bottom.

You will also need cleats—on the ceiling (for attaching the top face frame) and on the side walls (where the side face frames will be attached). Rest the bookcase on the pedestal and, using a level, mark the ceiling where the front of the case meets it. Mark the side wall where the front of the case meets it. Remove the bookcase and snap chalk lines along these marks (see page 104).

Nail a 2 × 4 cleat along the ceiling, into the joists, so the front edge of the cleat is flush with the marked line. Nail a 1 × 4 cleat into the side wall, through the wall framing, so the front of the cleat is flush with the marked line.

6 Install Bookcases

Place the bookcases on top of the pedestal and nail the cases into the wall through the nailer strips.

BOOKCASE WALL, SIDE VIEW

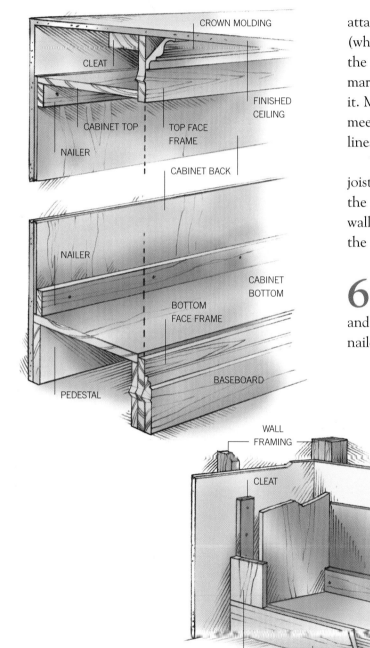

CROWN MOLDING
CLEAT
FINISHED CEILING
CABINET TOP
TOP FACE FRAME
NAILER
CABINET BACK
NAILER
CABINET BOTTOM
BOTTOM FACE FRAME
BASEBOARD
PEDESTAL

BOOKCASE WALL, INSTALLATION

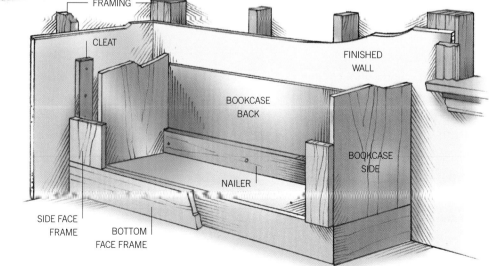

WALL FRAMING
CLEAT
FINISHED WALL
BOOKCASE BACK
BOOKCASE SIDE
NAILER
SIDE FACE FRAME
BOTTOM FACE FRAME

7 Cut and Install Face Frames

The face frames should be made of the same wood that was used to make the bookcases. Start with the bottom frame. If possible, use only one length of board to cover the front of the pedestal. The board should be about $\frac{1}{4}$ inch below the top of the bottom shelf so it does not create a lip. A 1 × 8 will be about right; if it does not quite touch the floor, the baseboard will cover any gap. Measure and cut the board, and nail it into the front of the pedestal.

The top horizontal frame board should cover the gap between the top of the bookcase and the ceiling, and overhang the bookcase slightly. A 1 × 6 should be sufficient. It can run continuously above a window to form a valance, or you can end it at the edge of the bookcase. Nail it into the ceiling cleat.

The vertical face frames will butt the top and bottom horizontal frames. First, measure the distance between the top and bottom face frames. This will be the measurement for all your vertical face frames. Next, measure any gap between the sides of the cases and the adjoining wall(s) and add about 1 inch to overhang the bookcase opening. If necessary, rip a 1-by board to the proper width. Cut the boards to the appropriate length and nail them into the side-wall cleat and into the side wall of the bookcase.

Attach a 1 × 4 vertical face frame to the other side of the case, flush with the edge if it flanks a window, or centered over the joint with another case.

Like a bookcase wall, a built-in cupboard or armoire would be integrated into a Colonial room by matching its moldings and paint color to what was used on the trim in the rest of the room.

8 Measure, Cut, and Attach Baseboard

Measure and cut the baseboard to cover the front of the bookcases (there will be a slight reveal above the baseboard), coping the ends that will meet the baseboard on adjoining walls. If the cases are separated by a window, run the baseboard along the sides of the cases and under the window; miter outside corners (see page 109) and cope inside corners (see page 110). Nail it into the pedestal.

9 Measure, Cut, and Attach Crown Molding

Measure and cut the crown molding to cover the top of the bookcases (see page 117). Wrap the molding around the cases and above the window, if applicable, using mitered joints at the outside corners and coped joints on the inside corners. Nail the molding into the top face frame and ceiling.

neoclassical

Whereas the Colonial style is perfectly suited to the more modest home, the styles of the next century are ideal for homes of a grander scale. From the mid-eighteenth to mid-nineteenth centuries, as a social hierarchy evolved in the colonies, there was a demand for homes that affirmed the status of their owners. This resulted in the progressively more imposing Georgian (1740–1790), Federal (1790–1830), and Greek Revival (1820–1860) styles, each borrowing ideas from its predecessor. The common theme was Neoclassical, a reinterpretation of Greek and Roman design elements.

The earlier Georgian homes were bold in their ornamentation, with deep moldings often painted in muted colors, then gilded. Later in the century, as trained architects began practicing in the colonies, the Federal movement brought a higher level of design and refined sophistication. Rooms were larger and more open. Doors and windows were elongated, and the trim work was more refined. Arched windows, curved bays, and semicircular fanlights above entry doors were typical of the period. In the Greek Revival home, pillars were used for framing or defining spaces both indoors and out.

There are distinct differences between the Georgian, Federal, and Greek Revival periods that are important if you are renovating a period home. But if you want to enhance a newer home that has high ceilings and large rooms (classical detailing may overwhelm small spaces), you can let personal taste dictate which classical ideas to incorporate within your own walls.

Here are some of the most interesting elements of the Neoclassical era.

DOORS Doors were always paneled; the ground-floor doors were tall and often double. The era brought the advent of French doors that led to back gardens. In Federal architecture, doors were often framed by flat Doric pilasters or fluted Ionic columns and painted to look like rosewood or mahogany.

WINDOWS Surrounds for windows ranged from the simplest fluted casing with corner blocks to a cornice trim cap to ornately carved entablatures. Often windows were inset into thick walls and had interior wood shutters that could fold flat against the inset. Window and door trim was generally painted white or a stone color.

BASEBOARDS In Georgian design, baseboards and chair rails were quite ornate. By the Federal

An ornate archway draws the eye upward. You can duplicate this look with prefabricated pilasters and arch trim.

CEILINGS White-painted plaster ceilings were standard in the average Georgian home. The ceilings in grander homes might have been divided into geometric panels surrounding a circular or rectangular centerpiece. Later Neoclassical ceilings were decorated with ornate plasterwork.

FIREPLACE SURROUNDS The most elaborate joinery in a Neoclassical home might occur around the fireplace. A common fireplace treatment could include a marble facing with fluted columns supporting a carved wood mantel shelf. The frieze might be decorated with a molded center panel, dentil work, or applied motifs.

period, baseboards were often composed of an 8-inch-high plank capped with a molding, which was either elaborately carved or painted with a faux finish.

WALL TREATMENTS Both wall frames and full wood paneling appeared in Neoclassical homes. After the middle of the eighteenth century, wood wainscot was limited to the dado area. During the Georgian era, stucco ornamentation—often gilded—was used to decorate the plaster walls. Muted colors of paint or wallpaper covered the walls of the grander Federal homes.

CORNICES A common Georgian treatment was to have a simple wood cornice molding carved with classical motifs supported by a dentil, ribbed, or egg-and-dart block below. In the Federal period, cornices were plain or decorated with motifs such as flowers and leaves, urns, or Greek key patterns. In the grandest homes, the cornice area was decorated with elaborate plasterwork that featured swags, urns, garlands, and other ornamentation.

Top From the fireplace to the wall, the doorway to the ceiling, trim was used to enhance every feature of a Neoclassical home.

Bottom Pediments and columns give scale to a high-ceilinged room. However, these Neoclassical elements can be used in even a lower-ceilinged room; see the projects on pages 50 and 76.

neoclassical projects

Most 8-foot ceilings cannot support the height and scale of elaborate, built-up Neoclassical trim treatments. But that doesn't mean you can't create Neoclassical style in a home with average ceiling heights. You just need to scale your design to the size of your rooms. We have designed two door and window surrounds that suit most rooms with 8-foot ceilings, as well as a more ornate treatment for higher ceilings. Also included are ideas for baseboards, a chair rail, and built-up crown molding to complement the surrounds.

There are many prefabricated fireplace surrounds in wood, marble, and cast stone that complement any Neoclassical decor. Most can be special ordered to fit around any brick projection or hearth. See Resources on page 126 to locate a manufacturer.

A carved, fluted, or gilded frieze turns the ordinary into the extraordinary. To incorporate this high style into your projects, substitute ornamental frieze boards for the plain ones in the fireplace surround on page 32 and the door surround opposite.

PROJECTS IN THE NEOCLASSICAL STYLE

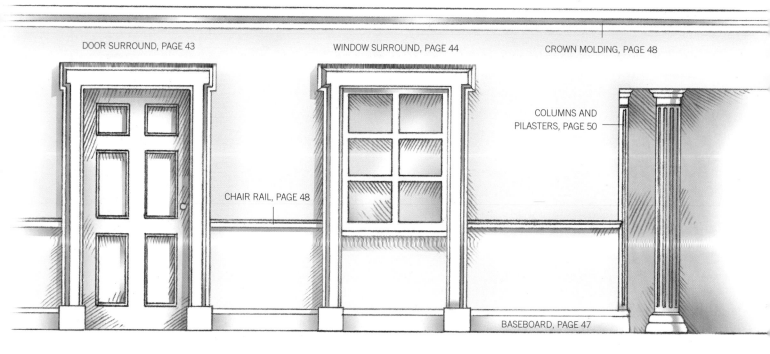

DOOR SURROUND, PAGE 43

WINDOW SURROUND, PAGE 44

CROWN MOLDING, PAGE 48

COLUMNS AND PILASTERS, PAGE 50

CHAIR RAIL, PAGE 48

BASEBOARD, PAGE 47

Door Surround with Fluted Casing

This door surround consists of two plinth blocks, fluted casing, and a built-up header. We suggest plinth blocks finished with chamfered edges; for additional decoration, you can purchase plinth blocks to match your baseboard detailing.

materials

- $1" \times 4\frac{1}{2}" \times 7\frac{1}{4}"$ plinth blocks
- $^{11}/_{16}" \times 4\frac{1}{4}"$ fluted casing
- 1×8, for frieze board
- $^{7}/_{16}" \times 1\frac{1}{16}"$ doorstop molding
- $1\frac{1}{8}" \times 1\frac{3}{16}"$ crown molding
- $\frac{3}{8}" \times 2\frac{1}{8}"$ lattice

1 Mark Reveals and Set Plinth Blocks
Mark ¼-inch reveals on the front faces of the side and head jambs (see page 106). Nail the plinth blocks to the bottom of the doorjamb and wall, with their inside edges ⅛ inch from the inside of the jamb.

2 Install Side Casings
Measure the distance from the top of the plinth block to ¼ inch above the bottom of the head jamb. Cut two lengths of fluted casing to that measurement. Center the pieces on top of the plinth blocks and nail them to the wall, making sure that the inside edges are on the reveal you marked on the jamb.

3 Cut Frieze Board
Construct the built-up header on your worktable, then attach it. First, measure the distance between the outside edges of the side casings. Cut a 1 × 8 frieze board to that length. Cut a piece of doorstop molding to that length plus ¾ inch; round off and sand the ends. Position the frieze board on top of the doorstop molding, centering it; glue and nail the two pieces together.

Project continues >

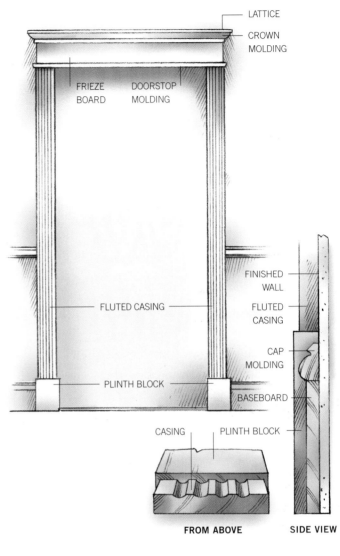

LATTICE
CROWN MOLDING
FRIEZE BOARD
DOORSTOP MOLDING
FLUTED CASING
PLINTH BLOCK

FINISHED WALL
FLUTED CASING
CAP MOLDING
BASEBOARD

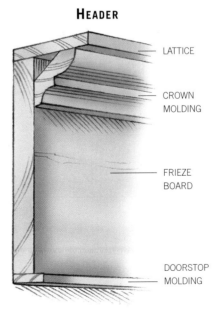

CASING   PLINTH BLOCK

FROM ABOVE   **SIDE VIEW**

HEADER

LATTICE
CROWN MOLDING
FRIEZE BOARD
DOORSTOP MOLDING

4 Attach Crown Molding to Frieze Board

Measure and cut the crown molding, mitering and returning the ends (see page 111) so the bottom edge is the same length as the frieze board. Center the crown molding on top of the frieze board; glue and nail the two pieces together.

5 Add Lattice

Measure the crown molding, then cut the lattice about ¾ inch longer. Position the lattice flat on the top of the crown molding, centering it; attach it with glue and nails.

6 Attach Header

Position the built-up header on the wall, its base along the top reveal line that you drew earlier. Clamp the header in place, then nail it into the wall framing.

A common element—shelves of the same dimensions atop the entablatures—keeps different door surrounds from seeming too disparate.

CROWN MOLDING
LATTICE
FRIEZE BOARD
DOORSTOP MOLDING
FLUTED CASING
APRON
PLINTH BLOCK
BASEBOARD

Window Surround with Fluted Casing

materials

- 1" × 4½" × 7¼" plinth blocks
- ¹¹⁄₁₆" × 4¼" fluted casing
- 1 × 8, for frieze board
- ⁷⁄₁₆" × 1¹⁄₁₆" doorstop molding
- 1⅛" × 1³⁄₁₆" crown molding
- ⅜" × 2⅛" lattice
- ⅝" × 2⁷⁄₁₆" chair rail molding, for apron (see page 48 for profile)

Measure, cut, and install a stool if necessary (see page 114). Follow the instructions for the door surround, preceding; the window surround should reach to the floor. Make the window apron (see page 114), butting it into the side casings.

Door Surround with Wide Head

See also illustration, page 40, and photo, page 44

With its wide, built-up casing and overhanging header, this simple door surround provides classic elegance to any room. The treatment uses plinth blocks with chamfered edges, but you can choose blocks as decorative as you like. A decorative molding is attached to the surface of the casing.

materials

- 1½" × 6½" × 7¼" plinth blocks
- 1 × 6s, for casing
- 1½"-square filler block
- 1 × 2s, for trim
- ¾" × 1½" molded or stamped trim
  (see illustration, page 44)

1 Mark Reveals and Set Plinth Blocks
Mark ¼-inch reveals (see page 106) on the faces of the side and head jambs. Nail the plinth blocks to the bottom of the doorjamb and wall, with their inside edges ⅛ inch from the inside of the jamb.

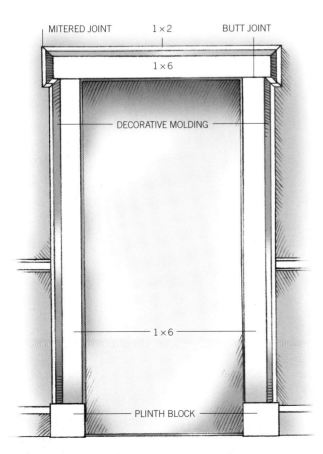

2 Install Side Casing
Measure the distance between the top of the plinth block and the horizontal reveal line; cut side casings to this length. Center them on top of the plinth blocks and nail them to the wall, making sure that the inside edges are as close as possible to the reveal you marked on the jamb.

3 Install Head Casing
Measure the distance between the outside edges of the side casings and add 3 inches. Cut a 1 × 6 to this length for the head casing. Center it over the side casings and nail it in place. Insert a 1½-inch-square filler block under the overhang on each side of the head casing.

CASINGS AND 1 × 2 TRIM

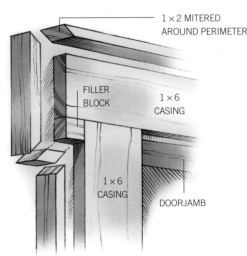

4 Install Perimeter Trim
The 1 × 2 trim will be installed with the 1-inch edge against the wall, so it projects ¾ inch in front of the casing. Measure around the perimeter of the casing—sides and head—and cut the trim to fit, mitering the corners (see page 109). Nail the trim in place.

Project continues ⇒

5 Attach Molded Trim
The decorative molding covers the joint between the casings and the 1 × 2 trim. Cut the trim to fit, mitering the corners. Nail the trim in place.

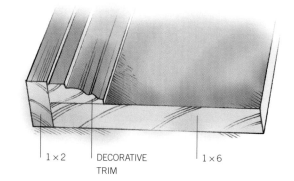

1 × 2   DECORATIVE   1 × 6
          TRIM

Window Surround with Wide Head

See also illustration, page 40

materials

- 1½" × 6½" × 7¼" plinth blocks
- 1 × 6s, for casing
- 1½"-square filler block
- 1 × 2s, for trim
- ¾" × 1½" molded or stamped trim
- ⅝" × 2⁷⁄₁₆" chair rail molding, for apron (see page 48 for profile)

Install a stool, if necessary (see page 114). Follow the instructions for the door surround, preceding; the window surround should reach to the floor. Make the window apron (see page 114), butting it into the side casings.

A classic door surround (like the project on the preceding page) can support a range of decorative entablatures; here the surround is topped with dentil detailing (opposite).

Dentil detailing gives elegance to doors as well as crown molding used on walls, cabinet tops, and fireplace surrounds.

Door Surround with Dentil Detailing

Dentil molding is a popular classical detail. This door surround, suitable for rooms with 9-foot or higher ceilings, uses prefabricated plastic crown molding that incorporates this dentil detail. You can buy such molding at home improvement centers; millwork suppliers may carry wood dentil or could custom-mill a similar molding for you. The dentil can also serve as crown molding.

materials

- $1\frac{1}{4}" \times 4\frac{1}{5}" \times 7\frac{1}{4}"$ plinth blocks
- $1\frac{1}{16}" \times 3\frac{1}{2}"$ molded casing (see page 46 for profile)
- 1×8, for frieze board
- $1\frac{5}{8}" \times 4"$ plastic dentil molding
- $\frac{3}{4}" \times 2\frac{5}{8}"$ cap molding (see page 46 for profile)

1 Install Plinth Blocks and Door Casing
Nail the plinth blocks to the bottom of the doorjamb and wall, with their inside edges $\frac{1}{8}$ inch from the inside of the jamb. Then measure, miter, and nail the side and head casings around the door (see page 112), centering the side casings over the plinth blocks.

Project continues >

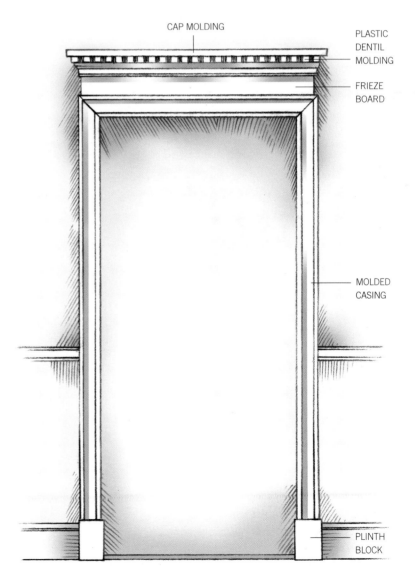

CAP MOLDING

PLASTIC DENTIL MOLDING

FRIEZE BOARD

MOLDED CASING

PLINTH BLOCK

2 Install Frieze Board

The frieze board is slightly thinner than the casings you have just installed, which means that the casing will project farther from the wall, creating a slight reveal. You want the edges of the frieze board inset from the casing edges by the same amount. Measure the distance between the outside edges of the side casings. Measure the reveal, multiply by two, and subtract this amount from the first measurement. Cut the frieze board to this length. Center the frieze board above the head casing and nail it into the wall.

3 Attach Plastic Dentil Molding to Frieze Board

Measure and cut the plastic molding, mitering and returning the ends so that the bottom edge is the same length as the head casing (see page 111). Attach the molding to the frieze board with construction adhesive and nail it in place.

4 Attach Cap

Measure the distance between the outside edges of the dentil molding, then cut a cap to that length. Run a bead of construction adhesive along the top edge of the dentil molding. Lay the cap on top of the frieze board and dentil molding. Nail it into the frieze board, then toenail it into the wall.

HEADER

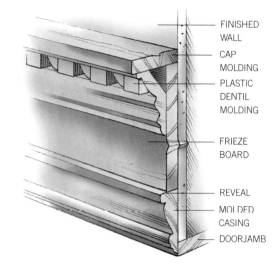

FINISHED WALL

CAP MOLDING

PLASTIC DENTIL MOLDING

FRIEZE BOARD

REVEAL

MOLDED CASING

DOORJAMB

Window Surround with Dentil Detailing

materials

- $1\frac{1}{4}" \times 4\frac{1}{5}" \times 7\frac{1}{4}"$ plinth blocks
- $1\frac{1}{16}" \times 3\frac{1}{2}"$ molded casing
- 1×8, for frieze board
- $1\frac{5}{8}" \times 4"$ plastic dentil molding
- $\frac{3}{4}" \times 2\frac{5}{8}"$ cap molding
- $\frac{5}{8}" \times 2\frac{7}{16}"$ chair rail molding, for apron

Measure, cut, and install a stool if necessary (see page 114). Follow the instructions for the door surround, preceding; the window surround should reach to the floor. Make the window apron (see page 114), butting it into the side casings.

upon reflection

Pilasters can turn a plain mirror into a work of art. To create this frame, purchase pilasters that coordinate with other trim in your home, matching their height to that of the mirror (this one runs from baseboard to crown molding, but it could start at the chair rail). Affix the mirror to the wall. Paint the backs of the pilasters black. Nail them into the wall on either side of the mirror, with their capitals slightly overlapping it.

The sides of staircase risers aren't neglected in a Neoclassical home. This is a good place for a wall frame or panel (see page 49) or a decorative appliqué. Whatever you choose should coordinate with other trim.

Baseboard

See also illustration, page 40

A typical Neoclassical baseboard is built up to give it height and style. Such a two-piece baseboard also provides versatility for meeting stairs or changing elevations. This baseboard is simple enough to work with a variety of door and window treatments. The baseboard should be thinner and shorter than the plinth block or door casing that it butts into (see illustration, page 41).

materials
- $\frac{1}{2}$" × $5\frac{1}{2}$" baseboard
- $\frac{9}{16}$" × $1\frac{3}{8}$" cap molding

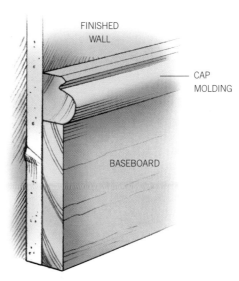

FINISHED WALL

CAP MOLDING

BASEBOARD

1 Install Baseboard
Measure, cut, and install the baseboard around the room, using butt joints (see page 108).

2 Install Cap Molding
Using the same measurements, cut and install the cap molding on top of the flat baseboard, using mitered joints on the outside corners (page 109) and coped joints on the inside corners (page 110).

Crown Molding

See also illustration, page 40

A single crown molding can serve as a simple treatment. If you have high ceilings or want your trim to impart a grander feeling, you can enhance the cornice by adding picture molding on the wall and panel molding on the ceiling. Paint all three moldings as well as the wall area between them a single color to create the effect of a large, built-up cornice. Or, for a more ornate effect, paint the moldings a color that is complementary to the lower wall, and paint the spaces between the moldings a third color.

materials
- $^{11}/_{16}$" × $4^{7}/_{16}$" crown molding
- $^{3}/_{4}$" × $1^{3}/_{4}$" picture molding, optional
- $^{3}/_{8}$" × $^{3}/_{4}$" panel molding, optional

1 Install Crown Molding
Measure, cut, and install the crown molding (see page 117).

2 Establish Panel and Picture Molding Lines
Draw or snap a chalk line on the walls $1^{1}/_{2}$ inches below the bottom of the crown molding and another line on the ceiling $1^{1}/_{2}$ inches beyond the top of the crown molding (see page 104).

3 Install Picture Molding
Measure, cut, and install the picture molding, using mitered joints on the outside corners (page 109) and coped joints on the inside corners (page 110). The top edge of the molding should be positioned on the line you snapped on the walls.

4 Install Panel Molding
Measure, cut, and install the panel molding, using mitered joints on the outside corners and coped joints on the inside corners. The inside edge of the molding should be on the line you snapped on the ceiling.

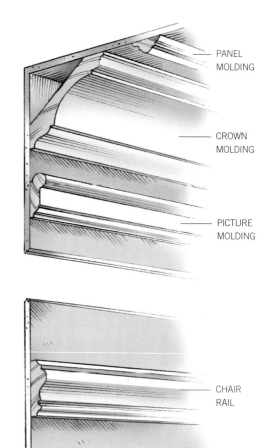

PANEL MOLDING

CROWN MOLDING

PICTURE MOLDING

CHAIR RAIL

Chair Rail

See also illustration, page 40

materials
- $^{5}/_{8}$" × $2^{7}/_{16}$" chair rail

Install the chair rail, butting it into the door and window surrounds (see page 116).

Decorative panels punctuate and add interest to blank stretches of wall. You can purchase paneling with raised sections and/or incised grooves; you can apply narrow trim in rectilinear shapes; or you can create the effect of paneling with molding-trimmed boards, as described below. Note in the photo how the edges of the panels parallel the wall's edges.

Wall Paneling

materials

- 1 × 4s
- ¾" × 2⅛" cap molding

Because of the ornate molding treatment used around the doors, windows, and ceiling, you don't need to decorate the walls. However, if you wish, you can create the effect of recessed wall panels by applying lengths of 1 × 4 vertically and horizontally on the wall. Apply the cap molding along the edges to create a more detailed recess.

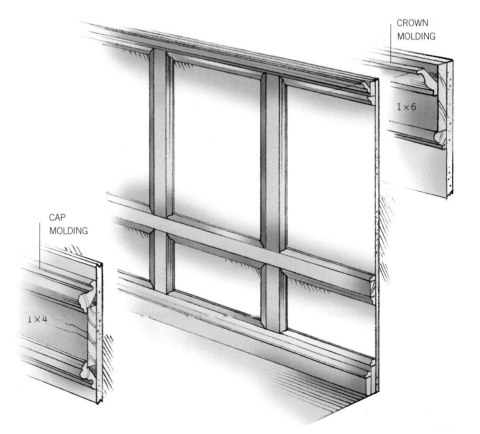

CROWN MOLDING

1 × 6

CAP MOLDING

1 × 4

A column is especially effective in a doorway capped with a built-up entablature (the projects on pages 41 and 45 lend themselves to this treatment). To wrap the end walls in pilasters, see the project on page 77; for the ornate effect in this photo, replace the 1 × 6 boards with 1 × 6 fluted casing.

Open Doorway with Columns and Pilasters

See illustration, page 40

You can soften and enhance an open doorway between two living areas with pilasters against the doorway walls and columns set just inside the opening. The size of the doorway and the scale of

your rooms will determine exactly how far apart the columns and pilasters should be set; you want to leave enough room to clean easily but not so much that a person could walk through the space. Try placing the columns a foot from the pilasters, then adjust as necessary.

These trim elements can be purchased prefabricated at home improvement centers and mill-work suppliers in a wide variety of styles. In selecting a pilaster, make sure its base is tall enough to match your baseboard.

materials
- prefabricated pilasters
- baseboard to match that in adjacent rooms
- prefabricated columns

1 Install Pilasters
Center the pilasters on the side walls of the doorway and nail them in place.

2 Install Baseboard
Run the baseboard around the bottom of each pilaster, connecting it to the existing trim. Use mitered joints on the outside corners (see page 109) and coped joints on the inside corners (page 110).

3 Mark Position of Columns and Cut to Fit
Prefabricated columns are usually sold in three pieces: a base, a shaft, and a capital. With some, the base and capital are made like sleeves to fit over the shaft and

hold it in place. Others require you to install the base and capital first, then fit the shaft between them.

Decide on the best position for the columns, and make marks on the floor that will be the center points of the bases. Then, using a plumb bob, mark the points that are straight above them on the ceiling. These will be the center points of the capitals.

4 Install Columns

Using the center points you marked, draw the outlines for the bases and capitals, making sure that one edge is parallel to the doorway wall. These will be your guidelines to ensure that they are straight.

For columns with sliding capitals and bases, measure the vertical distance between these two points. Cut the shafts of the columns to the measured height. Use L brackets to mount the shafts to the ceiling and floor. Use shims, if necessary, to level and create a tight fit. Slide the capitals to the ceiling and nail them in place. Slide the bases to the floor and nail them in place.

For three-part columns, first nail the bases and capitals in place on the floor and ceiling. Then measure the distance between the two and cut the shafts to fit. Shim the shafts for a tight fit and toenail them in place. Caulk any gaps.

INSTALLING A COLUMN

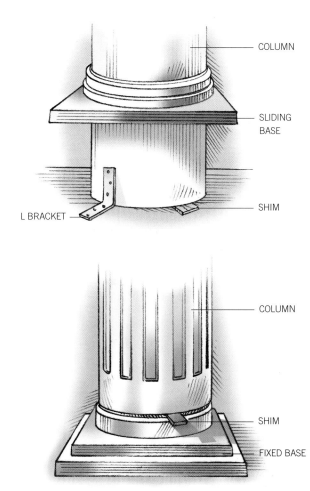

COLUMN

SLIDING BASE

SHIM

L BRACKET

COLUMN

SHIM

FIXED BASE

dressing up, up above

A purchased medallion can be simply a ceiling embellishment, or it can serve as an attractive base for a chandelier. Ceiling medallions are available in plaster, plastic, or wood; some come with an opening for a lighting fixture. If you are using only one medallion, center it on the ceiling. Apply the medallion according to the manufacturer's directions.

victorian

In the nineteenth century, the introduction of mass-produced materials, framed construction, and easily available American pattern books enabled builders to create more complex buildings. Features such as bay windows, towers, and decorative turnings characterized homes of the industrial age. Architects began to turn away from Neoclassical design in favor of more medieval and Gothic elements, and, as in the past, old design details were given a new interpretation. Often the ease of construction translated into excess, but the style had the advantage of offering a little something for everyone.

The Victorian period encompasses many different styles, the most familiar being Gothic Revival (1830–1875), Italianate (1840–1890), and Queen Anne (1870–1910). Gothic Revival has steep rooflines, gables, castlelike parapets, and lots of gingerbread trim. Italianate architecture is boxy, vertical, and symmetrical. In contrast, the Queen Anne style is asymmetrical, with a heavy use of towers, turrets, and wraparound porches.

Victorian trim is best saved for an authentic Victorian or Victorian Revival home. But the style is, by definition, eclectic and lends itself to individualism. Because it has no rigid guidelines, it is a style with which you can have some fun.

DOORS Double doors topped with transom lights or pediments often connected the public rooms in Victorian homes. Door surrounds were built up or created using simple molding and corner blocks with some kind of ornamentation. An open doorway could be transformed into an archway by the addition of ornate brackets in the top of the door frame (see page 56).

WINDOWS Stained-glass panels, especially above entry doors or windows, were popular during the Victorian era. Although ornamentation around the windows was heavy, the trim was based on personal taste rather than a strict style. In other words, anything was possible.

BASEBOARDS The high-ceilinged rooms demanded deep, molded baseboards, often with some kind of wainscot above.

WALL TREATMENTS Hardwood wall paneling signified wealth, especially when several kinds of hardwood were combined. In the late nineteenth century, full-height paneling or wainscot and chair rail were in vogue. Walls that were not covered in wood were painted or wallpapered; often several wallpaper patterns, separated by molding, were used on any

given wall. Wallpaper borders were also hung above the wainscot or under the cornice molding. In a Victorian home, the wood trim was either darker or lighter than the walls rather than the same color.

CORNICES Deep cornice molding was typically Victorian; 14-inch-deep, built-up cornices were common.

CEILINGS Gothic Revival ceilings were white with wood ribbing. In later Victorian homes, the most ornate ceilings were divided into rectangular or triangular sections, with molding, paint, and wallpaper defining the shapes. A plaster or painted rosette served as a stand-alone decoration or as a centerpiece for more exotic ornamentation. In the simplest Victorian homes, ceilings were painted white.

FIREPLACE SURROUNDS Although the fireplace itself had become smaller by the nineteenth century, it maintained its importance with the addition of a heavily decorated surround and overmantel. Mirrors were often centered in the overmantel and flanked by display shelves.

Opposite, top Decorative corner blocks come in a range of ornamental motifs that add interest to doorways and windows.

Opposite, bottom Molding in the Gothic style frames a bed in a nineteenth-century mansion. Today you may want to limit such fanciful decoration to a stylized bedroom or bath: You could use ornate brackets to frame a bed or window seat alcove or to hide a shower curtain rod.

Above Window surrounds with oversized corner blocks (a similar project is on page 55) and boxed ceiling beams (like the project on page 60) give scale to a room with high ceilings. The Victorian fireplace surround, with multiple display shelves and a mirror in the overmantel, provides an attractive focal point.

victorian projects

The Victorian trim elements here require a ceiling height of 9 feet or more. The reeded casing and corner blocks around the doors and windows, the bead-board wainscot, the picture rail, the crown molding, and the ceiling beams add the decorative quality that evokes the Victorian style. In old Victorians, it was typical to use wallpaper between the pieces of trim. You can replicate this effect by hanging one paper between the wainscot and picture molding and a complementary paper between the picture and crown moldings. You can also wallpaper the ceiling.

The side casings on this Victorian window have been extended to the floor (where they may butt into the baseboard or die into plinths) to frame a single recessed wall panel (see page 49).

PROJECTS IN THE VICTORIAN STYLE

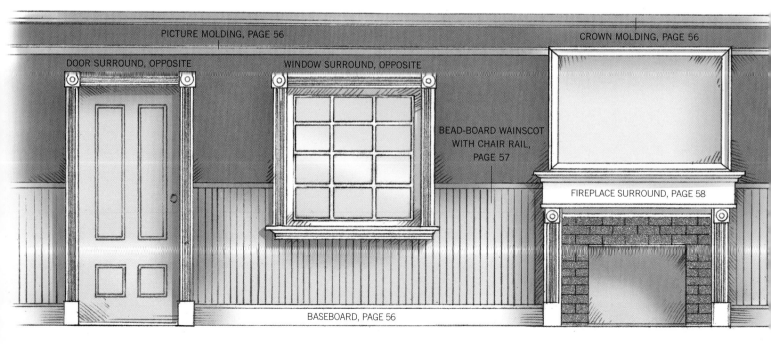

PICTURE MOLDING, PAGE 56

CROWN MOLDING, PAGE 56

DOOR SURROUND, OPPOSITE

WINDOW SURROUND, OPPOSITE

BEAD-BOARD WAINSCOT WITH CHAIR RAIL, PAGE 57

FIREPLACE SURROUND, PAGE 58

BASEBOARD, PAGE 56

Door Surround
See also illustration, opposite

The door surround features plinth blocks, reeded casing, and corner blocks. We use plinth blocks finished with chamfered edges, but you can select some that match the baseboard detailing if you want more decoration.

materials
- $4\frac{1}{2}$" × $7\frac{1}{4}$" plinth blocks
- $\frac{7}{8}$" × $4\frac{1}{2}$" × $4\frac{1}{2}$" corner blocks
- $\frac{11}{16}$" × $4\frac{1}{4}$" reeded casing

1 Mark Reveals and Set Plinth Blocks
Mark $\frac{1}{4}$-inch reveals (see page 106) on the faces of the side and head jambs. Nail the plinth blocks to the bottoms of the doorjamb and wall, with the inside edges of the plinth blocks $\frac{1}{8}$ inch from the edge of the jamb.

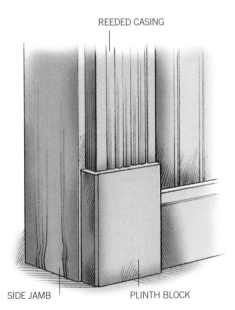

REEDED CASING

SIDE JAMB — PLINTH BLOCK

2 Measure and Set Side Casings
Measure each side of the doorway from the top of the plinth block to $\frac{1}{4}$ inch above the bottom of the head jamb. Cut the side casings to this measurement. Center the casings on top of the plinth blocks and tack them to the wall, making sure that their inside edges follow the reveal you marked on the jamb.

3 Attach Corner Blocks
Center the corner blocks on top of the side casings; glue and tack the blocks in place.

CORNER BLOCK

REEDED CASING

4 Install Head Casing and Nail Pieces in Place
Measure between the inside edges of the corner blocks. Cut the head casing to that size, making sure your cuts are square. Tack the head casing on the reveal line so that it fits without gaps but doesn't throw the corner blocks out of position. When all the pieces are properly positioned, nail them securely to the wall.

APRON PROFILE

Window Surround
See also illustration, opposite

materials
- $4\frac{1}{2}$" × $7\frac{1}{4}$" plinth blocks
- $\frac{7}{8}$" × $4\frac{1}{2}$" × $4\frac{1}{2}$" corner blocks
- $\frac{11}{16}$" × $4\frac{1}{4}$" reeded casing
- $1\frac{1}{16}$" × $3\frac{1}{4}$" casing, for apron

Measure, cut, and install a stool if necessary (see page 114). Follow the instructions for the door surround, above, but butt the side casings into the window stool. To install the apron, see page 114.

Baseboard

See also illustrations, pages 54 and 55

If you are installing a wainscot (see Bead-Board Wainscot, opposite), install the baseboard as part of that project.

materials

- 1 × 6s, for baseboard
- $^7/_{16}$" × $^3/_4$" base cap molding

To install the baseboard, see page 116. Measure and cut the base cap to fit on top of the baseboard, with coped joints on inside corners (see page 110) and mitered joints on outside corners (see page 109). Nail the baseboard in place.

SUITE OF VICTORIAN WALL TRIM

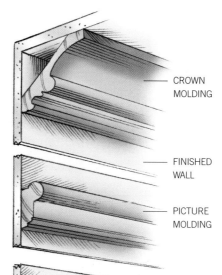

CROWN MOLDING

FINISHED WALL

PICTURE MOLDING

CHAIR RAIL

BEAD-BOARD WAINSCOT

BASE CAP

BASEBOARD

Picture and Crown Molding

See also illustration, page 54

materials

- $^3/_4$" × $1^3/_4$" picture molding
- $4^5/_8$" crown molding

To install the molding, see page 116. The picture molding should be 10 to 16 inches below the ceiling line. Connect the outer corners of the picture molding with mitered joints (page 109) and the inside corners with coped joints (page 110). Install the crown molding with mitered and coped joints (see page 117).

Rich color applied to crown molding, with wallpaper on both ceiling and walls, creates an appropriately elaborate treatment for a Victorian home.

do up a door

Adding ornamental brackets to a doorway can create an arched effect. Many types of wood brackets are available from Victorian trim and millwork suppliers. Case your door with a simple molded trim with mitered corners (see page 109), then center the brackets on the jambs in the doorway and nail them in place.

Bead-Board Wainscot

See also illustrations, pages 54 and 55 and opposite

Victorian wainscot differs from other wainscot styles in that the wood is usually stained rather than painted.

materials
- 1 × 6s, for baseboard
- ¼" bead-board plywood
- ⁷⁄₁₆" × ¾" base cap molding
- 2¼" × ⁹⁄₁₆" chair rail molding

1 Establish Chair Rail Height
Using a level, measure up from the floor about one third of the wall height (36 inches for a 9-foot ceiling). Draw or snap chalk lines (see page 104) for the entire wall to mark the top of the chair rail. If the floor is significantly off level, you may want to install the baseboard along a level line and use base shoe trim to hide the gap between the bottom of the baseboard and the floor (see page 107). However, if the floor slopes less than ¼ inch, you can install the baseboard along the floor and make the chair rail line parallel to it.

2 Install Baseboard
Install 1 × 6 baseboard around the room (see page 116).

3 Cut Bead Board
Measure and cut the sheets of bead board to fit the width of the walls. You may have to trim the height to fit between the baseboard and the chair rail line. Locate the studs (see page 108) and mark them just above the chair rail line.

4 Attach Bead Board
Apply construction adhesive to the backs of the bead-board panels, then press them against the wall. Nail the panels to the studs through the flat surface of the boards rather than through the beads.

Staining hardwood not only accentuates the natural grain of the wood and the pattern of the molding, it ties several different elements together.

5 Attach Base Cap
Measure and cut the base cap to fit on top of the baseboard; the cap will hide the intersection between the baseboard and bead board. Cope the joints on the inside corners (see page 110) and miter joints on the outside corners (see page 109). Nail the cap in place.

6 Attach Chair Rail
Measure and cut the chair rail (see page 116) and install it over the top of the bead board.

Fireplace Surround

See also illustration, page 54

This surround will work either for fireplaces that are flush with the wall or for those that have a masonry facing that projects from the wall. In steps 3 and 6, directions are given for both situations. You can complete the Victorian look by fitting a framed mirror above the mantel shelf.

materials

- 1 × 2s, for nailer and ledger strips
- 1 × 6s, for legs of surround and lintel
- 1 × 4s, for lintel, if necessary
- 1 × 12s, for frieze boards
- 1 × 8s, for mantel shelf
- ¾" half-round molding
- $1\frac{7}{16}$" × $1\frac{3}{4}$" bed molding
- $\frac{15}{16}$" × $4\frac{1}{2}$" × $7\frac{1}{4}$" plinth blocks
- $\frac{11}{16}$" × $4\frac{1}{4}$" reeded casing

1 Mark Clearance and Layout Lines
Following step 1 for the Colonial Fireplace on page 32, mark the clearance lines. Draw plumb (vertical) lines 5½ inches outside the side clearance lines. Draw a level (horizontal) line 13½ inches above the top clearance line.

2 Attach Nailer Strips
Measure the distance from the hearth or floor to the level line. Cut two 1 × 2 nailer strips to that length. Position one strip against a plumb line, extending toward the fireplace opening; nail the strip in place. Repeat on the other side of the fireplace.

3 Construct Box Legs for Flush Fireplace
For each leg of the surround, rip a 1 × 6 to 4¾ inches wide and another 1 × 6 to 4 inches wide. Cut these two boards, plus another 1 × 6, to the same length as the nailer strips. Following the leg detail below, nail the boards together to form a three-sided box.

Construct Box Legs for Fireplace Where Masonry Projects from Wall. To wrap the legs around masonry that projects from the wall, nail the 1-inch by 4¾-inch board and the 1 × 6 together as shown in the leg detail below. Set this L-shaped unit against the wall. If it is flat against the masonry, your leg is complete. Construct the second one to match. If there is a gap, measure it and rip two 1-by boards (one for each leg) to this measurement. Nail a ripped board into each 1 × 6 to create the inside return of the box.

4 Attach Legs to Wall
Position each leg on the wall so that the 1-inch by 4¾-inch board is tight against the outside edge of the nailer strip. Nail the board to the strip.

FIREPLACE FRAMEWORK

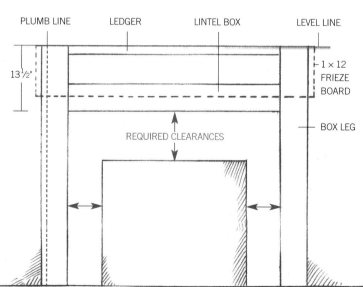

PLUMB LINE   LEDGER   LINTEL BOX   LEVEL LINE

13½"

1 × 12 FRIEZE BOARD

BOX LEG

REQUIRED CLEARANCES

LEG

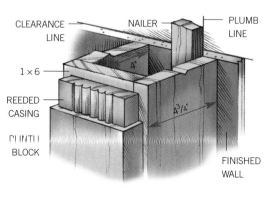

CLEARANCE LINE   NAILER   PLUMB LINE

1 × 6

4"

REEDED CASING

4¾"

PLINTH BLOCK

FINISHED WALL

5 Attach Ledger Strip

Measure the distance between the two legs. Cut a 1 × 2 ledger strip to this length. Nail it between the legs just below the level line you drew.

6 Construct Lintel for Flush Fireplace

Cut a 1 × 6 to the length of the ledger strip. Rip three 1 × 6s to 4 inches and cut them to the same length. Following the mantel detail above, nail the boards together to form a four-sided lintel box. Position it between the legs, with its bottom edge on the clearance line.

Construct Lintel for Fireplace Where Masonry Projects from Wall. If the fronts of the legs are against the masonry, cut a 1 × 6 to the length of the ledger. Apply mastic to the back of this lintel and position it between the legs, with its bottom edge on the clearance line. Toenail the lintel into the legs.

If there is a gap between the masonry and the front of the legs, measure it. Rip two 1 × 4s to this measurement minus $\frac{3}{4}$ inch, then cut the boards to the length of the ledger. Rip a 1 × 4 to 4 inches. Cut this, plus a 1 × 6, to the length of the ledger. Following the mantel detail above, build a lintel box with these four boards. Nail it in place.

7 Install 1 × 12 Frieze

Measure around the surround from one wall, across the front, and back to the other wall. Cut 1 × 12s to fit, mitering the corners (see page 109). Position them with their top edges flush with the tops of the legs. Glue and nail them into the legs and lintel.

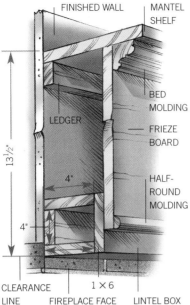

MANTEL

FINISHED WALL

MANTEL SHELF

BED MOLDING

LEDGER

FRIEZE BOARD

13½"

4"

HALF-ROUND MOLDING

4"

CLEARANCE LINE

1 × 6

FIREPLACE FACE

LINTEL BOX

8 Install Mantel Shelf

Measure the length of the front of the frieze and add 4 inches. Cut a 1 × 8 to this length. Position it, centered, over the frieze. Glue and nail it into the ledger and frieze boards.

9 Add Moldings to Mantel

Measure around the frieze boards. Cut the half-round molding to fit around the bottom edge of the frieze, mitering the corners (see page 109). Nail in place. Cut the bed molding to fit just under the mantel shelf, mitering the corners. Nail in place.

10 Add Trim to Legs

With white glue, attach a plinth block to the base of each leg, covering the joint on the leg (see page 114). Cut two plinth blocks 2¼ inches tall, then attach one to each leg just below the frieze. Measure the distance between the top and bottom plinth blocks, and cut two lengths of reeded casing to this measurement. Center the reeded casings on the plinth blocks. Glue and nail the casings in place.

To make a fireplace surround more decorative, search trim catalogs for wooden appliqués you can add to the frieze below the mantel shelf.

Ceiling Treatment

See photo, page 53, for a similar treatment

Paneled ceilings were common in Victorian homes. The simplest way to create a paneled ceiling today is to purchase prefabricated panels, which come in wood, plastic, and even hammered metal. You just snap a layout on the ceiling, then install the panels according to the manufacturer's instructions. However, if you wish to build your own ceiling beams, follow these directions.

materials

- 1 × 8s, for perimeter
- 2 × 4s, for nailers
- 1 × 6s, for sides of boxes
- 1 × 4s, for bottoms of boxes
- ¾" × 4⅝" crown molding
- ¾" × 1¾" picture molding
- ¾" × 2⅛" cap molding

1 Paint Ceiling

If you are going to paint the ceiling rather than wallpaper it, you may want to do that before you start. You may have to touch up the paint at the end of this project, but that should be easier than painting each individual panel.

2 Create Layout on Ceiling

Measure the length and width of the ceiling and divide it into even squares or rectangles that complement the size and shape of the room. Allow 5¼ inches for the beams that divide the squares. Make sure your layout accommodates any ceiling light fixtures. For instance, if you have a center fixture, you might want to create a large square around it, then break the rest of the ceiling into smaller, equal squares. Mark the ceiling to indicate the center point of each beam. Snap chalk lines (see page 104) 1¾ inches on either side of the center points to mark the edges of the nailers.

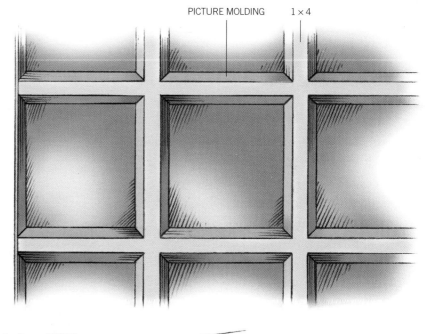

PICTURE MOLDING   1 × 4

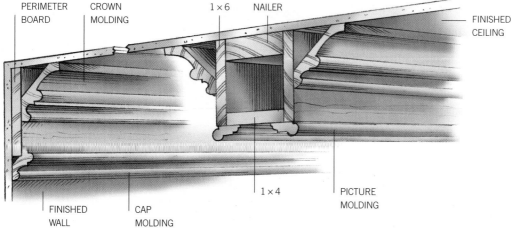

PERIMETER BOARD   CROWN MOLDING   1 × 6   NAILER   FINISHED CEILING

FINISHED WALL   CAP MOLDING   1 × 4   PICTURE MOLDING

3 Install Perimeter Boards and Nailers

Measure and cut 1 × 8 perimeter boards to run along the tops of the walls. Nail the boards in place. Measure the distance between the perimeter boards for the lengthwise beams, and cut 2 × 4 nailers to this measurement. Position the nailers between the chalk lines you've snapped on the ceiling and nail them in place.

4 Install Lengthwise Boxed Beams

Cut 1 × 6s to the lengthwise measurements, two for each beam. Nail pairs of boards into the sides of the nailers, butting them into the walls. Cut 1 × 4s to the same length, one for each beam. Construct the bottoms of the boxed beams by inserting the 1 × 4s between the 1 × 6s. Nail the boards together.

5 Install Cross Beams

Construct the cross beams in the same manner as the boxed beams, proceeding one panel at a time, butting the cross beams into the lengthwise beams and the walls.

6 Trim Beams

Measure around the inside of each square you have created, and cut the crown molding to fit, mitering the corners at each intersection (see page 109). Nail in place. Measure the bottom edges of each beam. Cut picture molding to fit around each square, mitering the corners. Nail in place.

7 Install Cap Molding

Measure, cut, and miter cap molding to run around the perimeter of the room, covering the bottoms of the 1 × 8 boards (see page 116).

Here, a modern living room becomes cozier and more inviting with the addition of a boxed-beam ceiling like the project on these pages. This Victorian element is at home in a Contemporary house, in part because it is companioned by other stained trim such as the molding on the arched doorway.

arts and crafts

Originating in England, the Arts and Crafts movement (1890–1929) was a rebellion against industrialization, an attempt by upper-class intellectuals to renew respect for local craftsmen. Architecturally, the movement placed an emphasis on craftsmanship and the intrinsic beauty of the building materials, making a clear connection with the natural environment. Built-in furniture enhanced the trim work and minimized clutter within the house.

Across the ocean, the Arts and Crafts philosophy was reinterpreted, emerging in several styles, all related by their attention to finish detail.

Frank Lloyd Wright created the Prairie style—low, horizontal homes that mimicked the flatness of the prairies—for his affluent midwestern clients. California architects Charles and Henry Greene and Bernard Maybeck designed high-style homes with open spaces, exposed wood framing and joinery, and artistic trim, influenced by both Spanish and Japanese architecture. Anyone could get free plans for a Bungalow-style house and furniture in Gustav Stickley's *The Craftsman* magazine. The house, which featured a simple, one-story floor plan, could be built to suit any environment. Trim work was limited to the baseboards, windows, and doors, so the style— also known as Craftsman and Mission—was not beyond the reach of less-experienced builders.

Although true Arts and Crafts trim work requires a high level of joinery and fine materials to be most effective, the style can be adapted to enhance the interior of any home.

DOORS The trim used in the door surround could be molded but was more often made of flat board, stained and sometimes beveled smooth at the edges. In grander homes, wood—indigenous to the area, to emphasize the connection to nature—was used for the door and window trim and for built-in furniture. If the wood was not stained, it was painted white, sage green, or olive green. The workmanship of the door itself was often more important than

Opposite *Built-in window seats, benches, and half walls were defining characteristics of the Arts and Crafts style.*

Left *Painted wood trim becomes prominent when walls are painted a contrasting color. Here the horizontal lines typical of Arts and Crafts—in the window and door surrounds, crown molding, mantel shelf, and elsewhere—pull a large open floor plan together.*

Below *Simple lines and quality hardwood accentuate the fine craftsmanship of built-in cabinetry and high wainscot. (See a similar wall-treatment project on page 66.)*

the trim around it. Stained or leaded glass and unusually shaped muntins could turn a door into a work of art.

WINDOWS A typical Arts and Crafts window had several small panes topping a single large one. The wood window framing matched other woodwork in the house. Window seats, shelves, or cupboards were commonly built under windows in place of windowsills.

BASEBOARDS Like the door and window trim, baseboards were simple, often made of flat board.

WALL TREATMENTS It was common to cover walls with wood wainscot extending to 3 feet below the ceiling. The panels of the wainscot were often recessed rather than raised, or were formed by overlaying battens on a flat wood panel. The fanciest examples had darker wood inlay in geometric patterns.

Simple treatments included a plate rail along the top of the paneling. Wallpaper—often an artistic rendering of leaves or flowers—sometimes replaced the wainscot or was hung above it. If pilasters or columns were included in the design, they would be Doric or square. Hallways were decorated to match adjacent public rooms.

CORNICES Cornice trim, like the baseboard and door and window surrounds, was simple, whether molded or made of flat board.

CEILINGS The ceilings of formal rooms were lined with boxed beams or occasionally wallpapered. In Mission-style homes the beams were carved and the plasterwork was embossed.

FIREPLACE SURROUNDS Considered the central gathering place of the home, the fireplace or

hearth was given prominence. It was often faced with earth-colored or decorated tile, which may have been framed by a wood surround and topped by a mantel shelf. An elaborate wood or tile overmantel was common. In many Arts and Crafts homes, bookshelves or built-in benches framed the fireplace to create a comfortable inglenook.

arts and crafts projects

Architecturally, the Arts and Crafts movement focused on woodwork, using fine wood and elegant craftsmanship. The most popular woods included vertical-grained fir and oak, which were stained to highlight the grain.

The projects presented include door and window surrounds and a wall treatment with plate rail. Note that the Art Deco Crown Molding on page 73 can be converted to an Arts and Crafts ceiling treatment: Just stain the wood and stack the boards vertically with the 1-inch ends against the ceiling, as shown.

Because the actual dimensions of lumber are less than their nominal dimensions (see page 100), in several projects we recommend that, for a true Arts and Crafts effect, you get wide boards and rip them to the precise width called for.

A Modern inglenook is trimmed with the flat boards typical of the Arts and Crafts style.

CORNICE

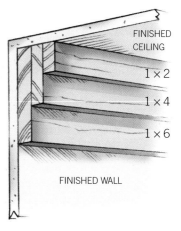

FINISHED CEILING

1 × 2

1 × 4

1 × 6

FINISHED WALL

PROJECTS IN THE ARTS AND CRAFTS STYLE

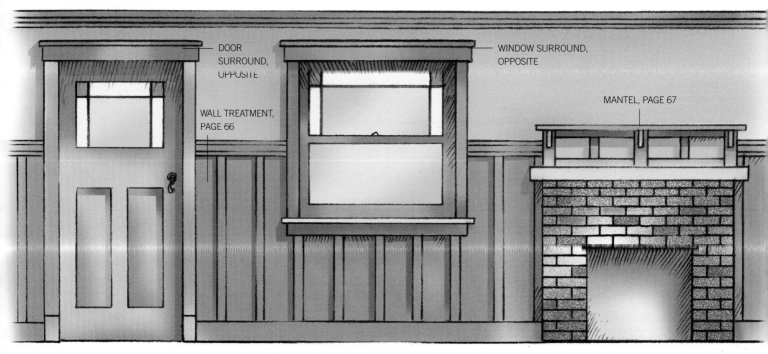

DOOR SURROUND, OPPOSITE

WINDOW SURROUND, OPPOSITE

WALL TREATMENT, PAGE 66

MANTEL, PAGE 67

Door Surround

See also illustration, opposite

materials

- $\frac{5}{4}$" × 4" × $7\frac{1}{2}$" plinth blocks
- 1 × 4s, for side casings
- $\frac{5}{4}$" × 4", for head casing
- 1 × 2, for head cap

Mark $\frac{1}{4}$-inch reveals (see page 106) on the faces of the side and head jambs. Nail the plinth blocks to the bottoms of the side jambs and wall, positioning their inside edges $\frac{1}{8}$ inch from the inside of the jamb.

Measure the distance from the top of a plinth block to the top reveal line. Cut the side casings to that measurement. Center the side casings on top of the plinth blocks and nail them to the wall, making sure that the inside edges follow the reveal you marked on the jambs.

Measure the distance between the outside edges of the side casings and add 1 inch. Cut a $\frac{5}{4}$-inch head casing to that length. Center it above the side casings and nail it into the wall.

Cut the 1 × 2 head cap the length of the head casing plus $\frac{1}{2}$ inch. Center the head cap above the casing and, with the narrow edge tight to the wall, nail it into the casing.

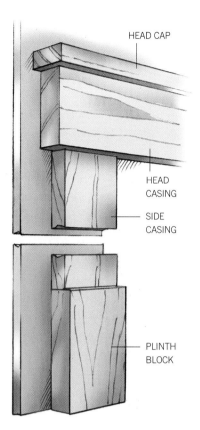

HEAD CAP

HEAD CASING

SIDE CASING

PLINTH BLOCK

Window Surround

See also illustration, opposite

materials

- 1 × 4s, for side casings and apron
- $\frac{5}{4}$" × 4", for head casing
- 1×, for stool
- 1 × 2, for head cap

Follow the instructions for the door surround, minus the plinth blocks. The side casings will butt into the stool. For the stool, measure the width of the side jamb (from window sash to interior wall surface) and add $1\frac{1}{2}$ inches. Rip a 1-by to this width. Measure the distance between the outside edges of the casings and add $1\frac{1}{2}$ inches. Cut the stool to this length. Sand the front and side edges of the stool, then install it (see page 114).

Make the apron (see page 114) from a 1 × 4, aligning its outside edges with the outside edges of the side casings.

Well-proportioned window surrounds and crown molding are elegant in their simplicity. Note that the step pattern of the crown molding is repeated at the top of the pass-through half wall— a fine craftsman touch.

Wall Treatment with Battens and Plate Rail

See also illustration, page 64

This project calls for battens applied directly to the wall. The battens should be made of good-quality wood and either clear- or dark-stained. The wall could be painted white for a true Arts and Crafts effect.

This wall treatment includes a plate rail that runs above the battens. If you plan to build the mantel (opposite), add the plate rail after you have installed the over-mantel shelf.

materials
- 1 × 6, for baseboard and plate rail base
- $7/16" × 2\frac{3}{8}"$ battens
- 2 × 2s, for plate rail support
- 1 × 4s, for plate rail

1 Establish Lines
Draw or snap chalk lines (see page 104) for the entire wall or room before starting this project so you can make sure the design is in balance. The first line will be 5½ inches above the floor, to mark the top of the baseboard. The second line will be 56 inches above the floor, to mark the bottom of the plate rail. The third

line will be 60 inches above the floor, to mark the top of the plate rail. All lines should be parallel and level. If the floor is way off level, install the baseboard along the level line, and use base shoe trim to hide the gap between the bottom of the baseboard and the floor (see page 107).

Locate the studs (see page 108) and mark their location on the wall above the 60-inch line. The battens should be spaced 12 inches apart on center. Plan their placement for the most attractive effect. You may want to start with a symmetrical placement under a window, for instance. Mark the batten locations.

2 Install Baseboard
Install the baseboard, using butt joints at the corners (see page 108).

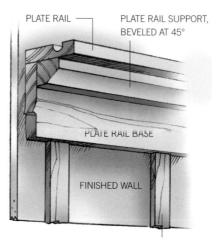

PLATE RAIL — PLATE RAIL SUPPORT, BEVELED AT 45°

PLATE RAIL BASE

FINISHED WALL

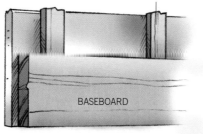

BATTEN

BASEBOARD

3 Install Battens
Cut unobstructed battens to 50½ inches long; for spots such as under a window, measure and cut the battens to fit. Glue the battens to the wall centered on the lines you have marked, and secure them with finish nails.

4 Create Base for Plate Rail
Rip 1 × 6s to 4 inches to make the base of the plate rail. Measure the distance around the room and cut the boards to fit. With the boards butted against the battens, nail the boards in place, connecting at corners with butt joints.

Bevel a 45-degree chamfer on one edge of the 2 × 2s. Cut the beveled 2 × 2s to length to fit around the room as plate rail supports. Position them on the plate rail base as shown, with the top edges flush, connecting at the corners with mitered joints (see page 109). Glue and nail the boards in place.

5 Build Plate Rail
Rip the 1 × 4s to 3 inches to create the plate rail. Rout a ½-inch groove in the boards about ¾ inch from the front edge. Position the boards on top of the plate rail base, mitering all joints. Nail the boards into the base.

Mantel

See also illustration, page 64

If you have a plain brick fireplace facade, you can create a simple mantel topped by an overmantel with a shelf that will increase the scale of your fireplace and complement the wall treatment. Establish the location of the overmantel shelf based on the height of the existing fireplace surround and that of the plate rail; it should rise a pleasing distance above the plate rail. If your existing fireplace surround is higher than the top of the plate rail, this treatment may be too much; a simple wood mantel or tile surround may be more appropriate.

materials

- 4 × 8, for mantel shelf
- 1 × 4, for verticals and ledger
- ½" × 2½" battens
- 2 × 4, for knee braces
- 1 × 6, for overmantel shelf

1 Establish Overmantel Shelf Height

Determine the most appealing height for the overmantel shelf and draw a line on the wall where you want it to sit.

2 Attach Mantel Shelf

The 4 × 8 should be of the same wood as any paneling in the room, or similar to it. Measure and cut the mantel shelf so its projection to the sides of the

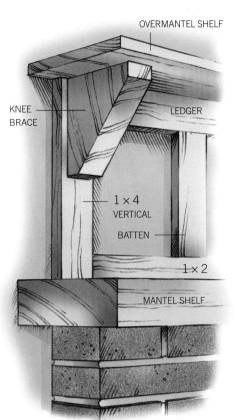

OVERMANTEL SHELF

KNEE BRACE

LEDGER

1 × 4 VERTICAL

BATTEN

1 × 2

MANTEL SHELF

brick facade is the same as its projection in front of it. Sand all exposed edges, softening the corners. Glue the mantel on top of the facade and toenail or screw it into the wall framing from the top, countersinking and plugging the screws.

3 Install Verticals

Measure the distance between the mantel and the shelf line you marked. Cut two pieces of 1 × 4 to this length. Position them on top of the mantel with the outside edges flush with the outside edges of the brick facing. Nail them into the wall. Cut a

third 1 × 4 board 3½ inches shorter and nail it into the wall, equidistant from the outside verticals and butting into the mantel shelf.

4 Install Horizontals

Cut a 1 × 4 ledger to fit between the two outside verticals, aligning all top edges. Nail the ledger into the wall framing. Rip a 1 × 4 to 2 inches wide. Cut two pieces to fit between the outside and middle verticals. Position each piece on edge against the mantel shelf and nail them into the wall framing.

5 Install Battens

Measure and cut two battens to run between the 1 × 2 strips and the ledger, centering the battens between the 1 × 4 verticals. Nail the battens into the wall.

6 Install Knee Braces

From the 2 × 4, cut three knee braces, as shown. Center the braces over the 1 × 4 verticals, with their tops aligned with the top edge of the ledger. Nail them into the 1 × 4s.

7 Install Overmantel Shelf

Measure the distance between the outside edges of the verticals and add 4 inches. Cut the 1 × 6 to this length, then sand its front and side edges. Position this overmantel shelf on top of the knee braces and nail it down into the braces.

From the boxed-beam ceiling, the eye travels down to rest on the beautifully crafted display cases and paneling. The stained trim and built-ins and dark leather sofa work together to create a harmonious environment.

Boxed-Beam Ceiling

Designers of Arts and Crafts homes often boxed exposed ceiling beams in formal rooms. To create this effect, we suggest installing simple false boxed beams. The exposed side of each board should be stained before the boards are installed. Boxed beams generally run the width of a room rather than along its length.

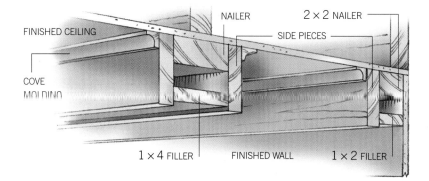

FINISHED CEILING

NAILER

2 × 2 NAILER

SIDE PIECES

COVE MOLDING

1 × 4 FILLER

FINISHED WALL

1 × 2 FILLER

materials

- 2 × 4s, for nailers
- 2 × 2s, for half beams
- 1 × 4s, for sides and fillers
- 1 × 2s, for half-beam fillers
- ¾" cove molding

1 Create Layout on Ceiling

If you are running the beams parallel to the ceiling joists, the easiest way to attach them is directly into the joists. If your layout does not allow this, you will have to install backing between the joists, above the ceiling, which requires opening up the ceiling or climbing into the attic above the room. In this case, you might want to hire a professional. If you are running the beams perpendicular to the joists, you will be able to attach them directly into the joists at the points where they intersect.

Locate and mark the joists (see page 108). Measure the length of the ceiling and divide it into equal units, each approximately 48 inches wide. You will install a half beam at each end and separate the sections with 5-inch beams. Mark the centers of the beams, then mark and snap chalk lines $1\frac{3}{4}$ inches on either side of the center lines (see page 104).

2 Install 2 × 4 Nailers

Measure the width of the ceiling and cut one 2 × 4 to this length for each beam. Cut two 2 × 2s to this length, one for each half beam. Position the 2 × 4s between the snapped chalk lines, and nail

them into the ceiling joists or backing. Nail the 2 × 2s against the end walls.

3 Install 1 × 4 Sides

For each beam, cut two 1 × 4s to the same length as the nailers. For each half beam, cut one 1 × 4 to the same length as the nailers. Nail a 1 × 4 into each side of each 2 × 4 nailer, and nail one 1 × 4 on the outside of each half beam.

4 Install 1 × 4 Fillers

For each beam, cut one 1 × 4 to the same length as the nailers. Insert these fillers between the 1 × 4 side pieces, either flush with the bottom edges of the sides or inset $\frac{1}{4}$ inch. Nail through the side pieces. For the half beams, cut 1 × 2s to the same length as the nailers and insert them between the wall and the 1 × 4s.

5 Install Cove Molding

Cut two lengths of cove molding for each beam (one for each half beam) to the length of the nailer. Position the molding tightly against the ceiling and the outside edges of the beams and nail it in place.

arts and crafts, easily

A flat cabinet door or end panel takes on Arts and Crafts style with the addition of 1 × 1 battens. Cut the battens 1 to 2 inches shorter than the dimensions of the door or panel. Position them 3 to 4 inches from the edges. Glue and nail in place.

modern

Modernism, which was in vogue between 1920 and 1950, had a strong effect on later architecture. It was a movement that encompassed the Art Moderne and Art Deco styles of Europe, both of which favored angular ornamentation applied to flat surfaces, such as the popular stepped-back pattern (see pages 72–74). A dramatic departure from the past, Modernism was a movement during which trim almost disappeared in favor of pure architectural form. Homes had open floor plans and huge, untrimmed, single-paned windows that were flush with the interior walls. The clean lines were elegant, but the style required expensive building materials and careful workmanship that was costly. In the tract homes of this period, therefore, trim was used sparingly.

A new Contemporary style that evolved in the late 1960s reflected a respect for the environment. Materials such as wood, stone, brick, and tile, evoking the natural world, were used both inside and outside the house. Cathedral ceilings and large picture windows created drama and required no further decoration. In these Contemporary homes, the trim consisted of clear-stained or whitewashed wood planks, and it was limited to the baseboards and window and door surrounds. Fireplaces were often left unframed, with a simple plank mantel extending from the wall above the fireplace opening.

Beginning in the 1980s, designers and builders began reviving and reinterpreting earlier Colonial, Georgian, Arts and Crafts, and regional designs, in the process dispensing with hard-and-fast rules about what kind of trim should be used. Decoration today is more playful, blending classical motifs with contemporary ideas. For instance, a square column might be topped by a round cylinder—or vice versa. Odd-shaped pediments might be placed over doors and windows. Instead of picture molding, copper tubing could serve as a support for paintings and artifacts. In this anything-goes mood, the traditions of the past may appear in pure form, may be combined in an eclectic style, or may be transformed almost to invisibility.

This Contemporary living room borrows ideas from early-twentieth-century design. Arts and Crafts–inspired battens break the long expanses of horizontal trim below the clerestory windows and on the fireplace surround. The stepped crown molding is a Modern adaptation of earlier Art Deco trim (see project on page 73).

Sleek columns, a curved staircase, and a round table contrast with the verticality of flat door and niche casings and wall paneling in this Modern home. Space, proportion, and surface are critical elements of the Modern movement in architecture.

Above A simple length of horizontal trim gives human scale to oversized windows and provides a mount for decorative drapes. With the addition of two vertical 1 x 4s, the trim also creates an attractive overmantel.

Right This Modern adaptation of a classical column proves that trim can be playful as well as functional. The column conceals a metal chimney flue; the rounded doorway and window to its right camouflage a dog bed.

modern projects

The projects presented on the following pages range from enhancing the plain clamshell door and window moldings of the 1960s to a suite of Art Deco trim treatments, from a Modern adaptation of a Federal door surround to a marriage of traditional crown molding and concealed strip lighting. As these last two projects demonstrate, today's Contemporary architecture borrows freely from past styles, so you may find that many projects from previous pages are appropriate in a Contemporary house.

Art Deco Door Surround

materials
- ⅝" × 2¼" step casing

Measure the door, then cut and install the casings, connecting them with mitered corners (see pages 109 and 113).

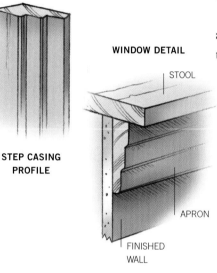

STEP CASING PROFILE

WINDOW DETAIL

STOOL

APRON

FINISHED WALL

Art Deco Window Surround

materials
- ¾" window stool
- ⅝" × 2¼" step casing

Install a manufactured window stool, wide enough to fit the thickness of the wall and project 1⅜ inches beyond it (see page 114).

Measure the window, then cut and install the casings, connecting them with mitered corners (see pages 109 and 113). Make the window apron with the same step casing, aligning its outside edges with the outside edges of the window casing. Finish the apron ends with mitered returns (see page 111).

PROJECTS IN THE ART DECO STYLE

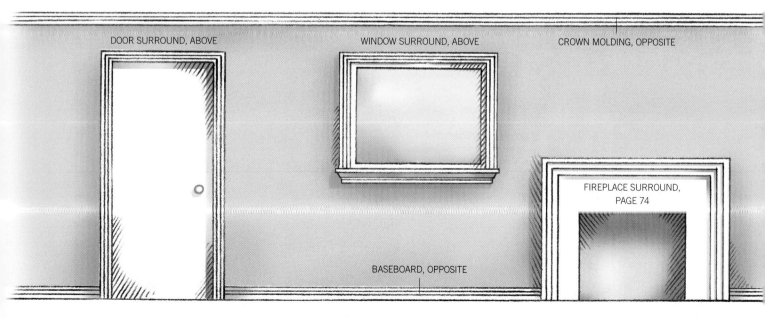

DOOR SURROUND, ABOVE

WINDOW SURROUND, ABOVE

CROWN MOLDING, OPPOSITE

FIREPLACE SURROUND, PAGE 74

BASEBOARD, OPPOSITE

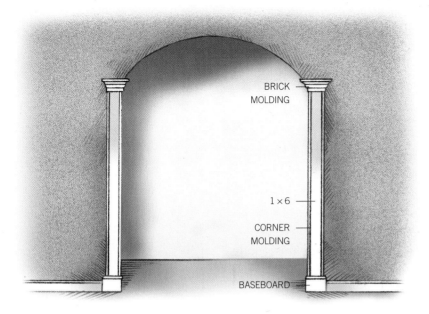

BRICK MOLDING

1 × 6

CORNER MOLDING

BASEBOARD

Simple columns soften a large doorway opening and provide stately elegance to this formal room. (To install columns, see page 50.)

Pilasters Flanking an Archway

An archway acquires a classical air when it is flanked by pilasters. For a Contemporary twist, however, there is no trim on the actual arch. The pilasters wrap around the three sides of the walls on either side of the archway (end walls). A simple baseboard with ogee detail runs around the entire room, also covering the bases of the pilasters.

materials

- 1 × 6s, for pilaster sides
- ¾" × 5½" baseboard
- 1¼" × 1½" brick molding
- 1¹⁄₁₆" corner molding

1 Install Pilaster Sides

Measure the distance between the floor and the point where the arch just begins its curve. Cut six 1 × 6s to this length (three for each side of the opening). Measure the width of the end of the wall, and rip two of the 1 × 6s to that width. Nail a ripped board to the inner face of each end wall. Butt a 1 × 6 on each side of the ripped boards and nail them in place.

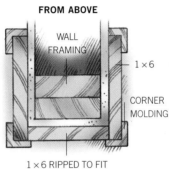

FROM ABOVE

WALL FRAMING

1 × 6

CORNER MOLDING

1 × 6 RIPPED TO FIT

BRICK MOLDING

1 × 6

CORNER MOLDING

BASEBOARD

2 Install Baseboard

Measure around the perimeter of the floor, including all three sides of each pilaster. Cut the baseboard to fit, mitering the corners (see page 109).

3 Install Pilaster Crown

Measure around the top of the pilasters, then cut brick molding to fit, mitering the corners. Install the molding as you would crown molding. Finish the ends with mitered returns (see pages 109 and 117).

4 Install Corner Molding

Measure the distance between the baseboard and brick molding. Cut eight pieces of corner molding to fit. Nail into the four corners of each pilaster.

Backlit Crown Molding

By installing crown molding a few inches below the ceiling and hiding a strip of lights behind it, you add a modern function to a classical decorative treatment. This project uses strip or rope lighting, which requires its own electrical source. The strips are available either as 120-volt incandescent lighting or as low-voltage lighting. For 120 volt, you will probably need to install an outlet for the plug behind the crown molding, although some incandescent lighting strip systems can be hardwired—wired directly to the electrical source without using an outlet. For low-voltage lighting, be aware that the trans-

former it requires is too large to hide behind the molding. You will need to install it in another location, such as a closet, and run low-voltage wiring from it to the lighting strip. If you don't have experience installing a transformer or an outlet, hire an electrician.

Before purchasing all the materials, buy just enough to make your mock-up (see step 1). When you are sure of all the dimensions, purchase the required materials.

materials

- $^9/_{16}$" × $5^1/_4$" baseboard with ogee detail
- 2 × 4s, for nailer block
- strip or rope lighting
- $2^{15}/_{16}$" × $3^1/_{16}$" crown molding

1 Construct Mock-up

To determine the exact angle and placement of the crown molding, it is a good idea to create a mock-up using the three main wood elements: the ogee baseboard, crown molding, and 2 × 4. Cut a sliver of each element. Lay the baseboard (which will be used as a backer board to support the crown molding) on a worktable. Mark a reveal line $^1/_4$ inch from the molded edge (see page 106); butt the bottom edge of the crown molding against this line, and tack it in place. Place the 2 × 4 against the intersection of the first two pieces and mark on it the angle formed by the

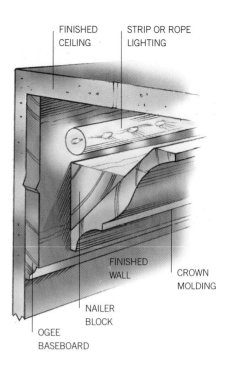

FINISHED CEILING

STRIP OR ROPE LIGHTING

FINISHED WALL

CROWN MOLDING

NAILER BLOCK

OGEE BASEBOARD

crown molding (the angle of the molding illustrated is 45 degrees). Rip the 2 × 4 along the angle line you have marked; insert it between the other two pieces, and tack it in place.

Position the mock-up on the wall, with the flat end of the baseboard tight against the ceiling. You may have to adjust the height of the reveal line or the size of the crown molding if the spacing isn't perfect. The top of the nailer block should be at least $2^1/_4$ inches from the ceiling to give adequate room for the strip lighting. The top of the crown molding should be far enough from the ceiling for maximum light to pass through the opening. Once you've established the correct placements, mark the bottom of the crown molding and the top of the nailer block on the baseboard.

Sconces below and backlit crown molding above provide attractive ambient light.

2 Mark Wall Studs

Mark the locations of the wall studs (see page 108) all along the wall, 6 inches below the ceiling.

3 Install Electricity

If you are using incandescent lighting, cut a hole for a new outlet just below the ceiling, where it will be concealed by the crown molding. Bring wires to this location. The outlet will be installed after you attach the backer board to the wall. If you are using low-voltage lighting, install the transformer in a convenient location and run wires to the molding area. Whether you use incandescent or low-voltage lighting, you will need to install a switch to turn the lights on and off.

4 Install Decorative Backer Board

Measure around the perimeter of the ceiling. Cut the baseboard to fit, mitering the corners (see page 109). Determine where the electrical wires will come through and cut a hole in the baseboard. Position the baseboard as you did in the mock-up, tightly against the ceiling, and nail or screw it into the wall studs. Paint or stain the baseboard. If you are installing an electrical outlet box, do it now.

Using your mock-up as a guide, mark two lines along the backer board—one for the top of the nailer block and one for the bottom of the crown molding.

5 Rip Nailer Block

Using the angle you established in your mock-up, rip 2 × 4s

Backlit crown molding adds to the drama of a room painted a powerful periwinkle.

to make the nailer block. You should be able to get two pieces of nailer block from each 2 × 4.

6 Prime Nailer Block and Back of Crown Molding

To maximize luminescence, the lighting strip should be surrounded by white surfaces. Prime the back of the crown molding and the exposed top of the nailer block before installing either.

7 Install Nailer Block

Position the nailer block along the line you marked, its angled side facing the floor. Nail it into the wall studs.

8 Attach Strip or Rope Lighting

Before installing the strip or rope lighting, you may want to test whether it provides better light attached to the wall or

attached to the top of the nailer block. Tack it first in one location, then the other, and hold a length of crown molding in front of it while the lights are turned on. Once you decide the best position for the lighting, follow the manufacturer's directions to attach the mounting clips. Press the strip or rope lighting into the clips, and connect it to the electrical source.

9 Install Crown Molding

Measure for the crown molding and cut it to fit, mitering the outside corners and coping the inside corners (see page 110). Nail the molding into both the backer board and the nailer block.

country

If you want to give your home Country character, the key is to focus on the small details, keeping everything simple. Function and livability took priority over status in early rural homes, and they are still important characteristics of the style.

COTTAGE

Cottage style, as we know it, is an adaptation of the earliest American building traditions, when settlers from humble backgrounds in England built houses patterned after the single-room cottages they knew from their homeland. As in England, their houses were timber framed. Here, however, they were usually covered in clapboards rather than stone or brick; wood was abundant, whereas the lime used to manufacture mortar was not as readily available.

Today's Cottage style borrows much of its charm from early Colonial-era details, such as those found in American saltbox and Cape Cod cottages. Modern cottages may not be as small as their predecessors, but they are still no larger than necessary, with well-crafted detailing that is never conspicuous. The style is typified by walls covered in bead board or tongue-and-groove wainscot that runs to the chair rail or ceil-

Throughout rural America, regional architecture reflects the cultural heritage, class, and building traditions of the immigrants who settled here. These newcomers combined their building experience with whatever materials were readily available to create homes that were distinctive in their construction, layout, and decorative finishes. Such homes, which were not designed by architects or meant to be design showcases, are admired for their simplicity, informality, and comfort.

It is just these characteristics that are drawing homeowners back to vernacular styles. Today's popular Country style is actually several styles, encompassing not only American regional design but also styles from all over Europe. Rich in detail, Country style is flexible enough to accommodate many individual preferences.

ing. The baseboard and any other trim should be simple, painted white or a color that reflects nature, such as blue or green. Some cottages have wood ceilings; others have open or boxed beams, which create a cozy, low-ceilinged effect. Interior wood shutters, painted white or the color of the trim, can add interest to windows.

FOLK

Folk architecture reflects the traditions and crafts of a community rather than the artistry and design of an individual. Passed down for generations through the community, the elements of Folk architecture are specific to a region.

The most influential Folk styles in America are Scandinavian, Shaker, and Southwestern—all uniquely based in the philosophies or crafts of their creators. The Scandinavians used simple trim, often with scalloped edges. They painted designs on their door and window casings, ceiling beams, and shelves. In fact, it sometimes seemed that they added wood trim just to have a surface on which to paint their designs.

Continues >

Opposite, top *A Victorian spandrel above a doorway takes on Cottage style when painted white.*

Opposite, bottom *Tongue-and-groove wainscot set at an angle achieves an informality that is decidedly Country.*

This page, top right *Stencil or paint a design above the chair rail to turn a Colonial or Neoclassical wall paneling into a Folk treatment.*

This page, above *Wood corbels are aligned with the window casings to support a deep windowsill that extends around this wood-lined Cottage bathroom.*

This page, right *In perfect Folk tradition, beds and windows are trimmed with wood cutouts and painted brightly.*

Trim is minimal in Southwestern style. Here, the beams are exposed, with a decorative corbel below one. If you simulate this ceiling with rough 4 × 4 beams, nail them into ceiling joists.

Shaker style, which became synonymous with simplicity, derived from a philosophy that everything in a house should be functional and efficient. Any ornamentation was deemed superfluous and ostentatious. Plain boards were used to cover the cracks between the walls, floor, and ceiling. A simple chair rail protected the walls from being marred by furniture. Walls were usually white, but trim could be painted one of a select number of approved colors, including blue, brick red, yellow-brown, and green. The Shakers also used pegs to hang clothing and keep unused chairs, tools, and other articles from cluttering the floor.

Both color and craft help define the Southwestern style, which combines Native American adobe construction with the more sophisticated building techniques of the Spanish colonial period. Today, the Southwestern style can be informal or refined, depending on whether the interior stucco walls are left rough or smoothed to a fine finish. Window and door openings are finished without trim, and the structural header is often left exposed. Rough-hewn or round ceiling beams (vigas) are left exposed on both the interior and the exterior of the house. If there is trim between the tile floor and plaster walls, it is usually made of ceramic tile. Any wood trim or accessories, including the occasional baseboard and crown molding, is frequently painted in multiple colors, adding a vibrant contrast to the cool white of the stucco walls.

RUSTIC

Rustic Country style is something of a catchall category, encompassing log cabins and bunkhouse designs, English Tudor, and rural French and Spanish influences. As with the Southwestern style, some or all of the structural framing of these homes is left visible, often replacing trim as the dominant decorative element. But, unlike Southwestern detailing, the wood is either stained or left unfinished.

Rustic style was first brought to America by immigrants from Scandinavia, who constructed half-timber and log homes. The style was popularized by the Scots and Irish in the backcountry areas they settled during the early eighteenth century. Tudor and Spanish influences include dark timber framing and ceiling beams that contrast with white plaster walls. From France and Italy the style takes whitewashed or light-

stained wood for door and window frames complemented by terra-cotta or earth-colored walls.

In reviving Rustic Country style, Americans have felt free to blend and elaborate on these elements. Trim work in the simplest log cabins might consist only of knotty pine door and window surrounds made of flat or rounded lumber with butt joints. More elaborate treatments use gnarled logs and branches to create staircase railings and banisters. Stripped, these logs are transformed into

Stripped branches form an attractive overmantel above a Rustic fireplace.

room dividers or columns to narrow wide openings between rooms. In European-style Rustic homes, plank or rough-cut wood baseboard covers the gap where tile floors meet walls. Rough boards applied to the surface of plaster walls suggest half-timber framing. Whitewashed wood may be substituted for the more traditional stone in fireplace mantels, shelving, and simple baseboard. Decorative corbels can support wood ceiling beams or be mounted on the walls and used as floating shelves. The details are Rustic, but the effect is new and fresh.

Above *Rough-sawn 4 × 4s serve as braces for exposed posts and beams; around the island, stained tongue-and-groove panels are set at an angle, bordered by battens and plinths, suiting Victorian trim elements to a Rustic interior.*

Left *In this blend of classical design elements with Rustic style, tree trunks serve as columns to support a large beam between rooms.*

A plate rail above the bead-board wainscot provides a place to set the knickknacks that are integral to Cottage design. You can create this wall treatment with the project below.

country projects

Many of the projects on the previous pages will suit a Country-style home. Colonial molded casings and baseboard, Arts and Crafts flat casings with butt joints, Victorian bead-board wainscot, and Arts and Crafts boxed beams take on a Cottage style when painted white or a light color. For a Rustic effect, doors and windows can be framed with knotty pine, using flat casings with a rounded edge, butt joints, and a clear finish.

On the following pages are projects that are specifically Country, including Cottage-style bead board with plate rail, a Shaker-style peg rail, a wood valance suitable for a Folk-style room, and a Rustic ceiling of boxed beams supported by corbels.

Cottage Paneling with Plate Rail

This wall treatment could be used to cover an entire room, or as wainscot along a single wall with the rest of the room wallpapered. Wainscots and plate rails are often painted white.

materials

- 1 × 6s, for baseboard and plate rail
- ¼" bead-board plywood
- 1 × 8s, for plate rail base
- 3½" × 6½" corbels
- 4¼" crown molding

1 Establish Plate Rail Height
Using a level, draw or snap chalk lines (see page 104) for the entire wall to mark the top of the plate rail, approximately 60 inches from the floor. Snap a second line 7½ inches below the first to mark the top of the bead board.

2 Install Baseboard and Bead-board Panels
Install the baseboard around the room (see page 116). Measure and cut the bead-board panels to fit around the room between the baseboard and the lower of the two lines you marked. Locate studs (see page 108) and mark them just above the plate rail line. Apply construction adhesive to the back of the panels and press them against the wall. Nail through the flat surfaces of the boards, not the beads, into the studs.

3 Install Plate Rail Base
Cut 1 × 8s to fit around the wall. Using a dado head on the table saw (or a rabbeting bit on a router), cut a ¼-inch × ¼-inch rabbet on the bottom back edge (see illustration, opposite) to fit over the top of the bead board. Fit the rabbet over the bead board, and nail the boards to the wall. Connect at any corners with butt joints (see page 108).

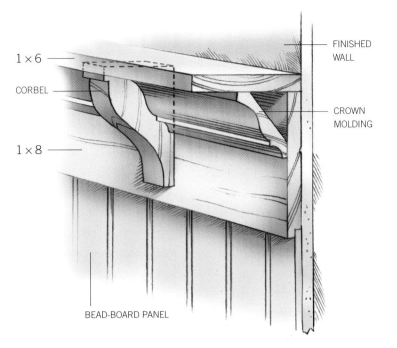

1 × 6

CORBEL

1 × 8

FINISHED WALL

CROWN MOLDING

BEAD-BOARD PANEL

4 Install Corbels

Install a corbel every 32 inches along the length of the plate rail base, with the tops of the corbels flush with the top of the 1 × 8. You can also put a corbel at the end of the run, next to a window or door casing, to avoid creating a return for the end of the crown molding (see step 6).

5 Cut and Install Plate Rail

Cut 1 × 6s to fit on top of the corbels. For more detail, you can rout the front and exposed side edges. Position each 1 × 6 with one edge snug against the wall and one side on the corbels; nail the 1 × 6s into the corbels and toenail them into the wall studs.

6 Install Crown Molding

Measure between the corbels, and cut the crown molding to fit. Make coped joints at any inside corners (see page 110) and mitered joints at any outside corners (see page 109). Where the crown molding meets window and door casings, finish with a mitered return (see page 111), or install another corbel.

do a dado

Designs cut out of sheets of laminated plywood provide a Folk-inspired dado treatment in a screened porch. If you're handy with a jigsaw, you can create your own decorative panels and use them in place of traditional wainscot or wall paneling.

3 Install Pegs
Mark a horizontal line centered top to bottom along the length of each 1 × 4. Mark the placement of pegs at equal intervals on the line. Clamp the board to a worktable, and on each mark drill a ¾-inch hole, either straight or at a 30-degree angle, halfway through the board.

If you are making your own pegs, cut dowels about 6 inches long. With sandpaper, round off the ends that will be visible.

With a small bristle brush, apply glue in the holes and around the ends of the pegs, then insert the pegs into the holes. If necessary, tap them in place with a hammer, using a wood block between the hammer and the dowel. Screw 1-inch by No. 6 bugle-head screws through the back of the board into the end of each peg.

4 Attach Board to Wall
Position the peg rail with its top edge along the level line, and nail it into the wall framing.

Above *A Shaker-style peg rail can be placed at chair-rail or picture-rail height—or both.*

Below *Pegs add utility to a Cottage-style shelf.*

Peg Rail
A peg rail can line an entire room or just a section of a wall. You can buy a prefabricated rail with decorative pegs, or make one yourself as described here. Peg rails can suit many different Country styles. Left plain or painted a solid color, they're Cottage or Shaker style; stenciled with a design, they become Folk. A rounded length of clear-finished knotty pine with crude dowels or twigs works well in a Rustic setting.

materials
- 1 × 4s
- ¾" wood dowels or Shaker-style pegs

1 Mark Wall
Mark a level line on the wall about 80 inches above the floor, or at the height of the top of the door. Locate the studs (see page 108); mark them above the line.

2 Cut and Prepare Backer Board
Measure the length of the wall or walls you want to cover, and cut 1 × 4s to cover the distance. You can bevel or rout the edges for more detail.

Wood Valance

See illustration, page 88

There are several ways a wood valance can add a decorative element to an otherwise plain room. The most obvious is over a window, to conceal the heading and hardware of a roll-up shade, blind, or curtain. But a valance can also hide a fluorescent light tube in a bathroom or kitchen, or screen the rings of a shower curtain. If you install the valance against the ceiling, you can run a flat board at the same height along the wall as a crown molding.

This simple project, painted to match the wall, will subtly dress up a room. However, with a design stenciled along its surface—and perhaps a scalloped pattern cut into its edge—it becomes a Folk treatment. You can continue the scalloped edge and/or stenciled design on the crown molding as well.

materials

- 4" metal angle brackets
- 1 × 8s
- ¾" cove molding
- ⁷⁄₁₆" × 1¼" doorstop molding

1 Determine Dimensions and Mark Lines
The width of the valance will depend on the size of what you are covering. Over a window, the valance should be at least 1 inch wider than the window, the window treatment (such as draperies), or any hardware. It should also be at least half an inch deeper than any hardware. Mark the outside edges of the valance on the wall. For its height, mark a level line 5 inches above the window opening.

Project continues >

FOLK-STYLE VALANCE

window dressing

Give Folk style to a window by applying stenciled wood shelf brackets to its corners. Center 1-inch-thick brackets on the window jambs and toenail them in place. Case the window with a molded trim with mitered corners.

2 Install Angle Brackets

Locate the wall framing above the window that you can screw into (see page 108). Position a 4-inch angle bracket with its top edge along the level line where you can screw into the framing, no more than a foot from the end of the valance. Screw the bracket into the wall framing with 1½-inch screws. Repeat at the other end of the valance. The valance needs support at least every 40 inches; if necessary, install a third bracket in the middle.

3 Build Valance

Cut a 1 × 8 to fit between the outside edge marks; this will be the top of the valance. Sand the edges. Cut a second 1 × 8 board 3 inches shorter than the first; this will be the front of the valance. On a worktable, butt one edge of the front against one side of the top 1½ inches from one long edge and centered left and right. Nail the pieces together to form an L shape.

Measure from the inside edge of the front to the other long edge of the top. Cut two 1 × 8s to this measurement; these will be the sides. Position the sides against the front, flush with its outside edges, to form a three-sided box. The top will overlap the front and sides by 1½ inches. Nail the sides in place.

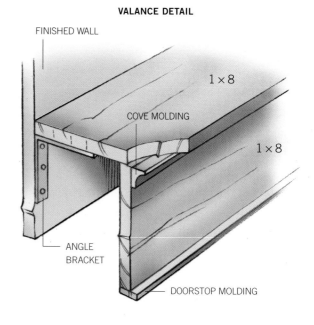

VALANCE DETAIL

FINISHED WALL

1 × 8

COVE MOLDING

1 × 8

ANGLE BRACKET

DOORSTOP MOLDING

Measure the distance around the box. Cut cove molding to fit under the overhang, mitering the corners (see page 109). Nail it in place. Cut doorstop molding to fit around the bottom of the front and sides, mitering the corners, then nail in place.

4 Install Valance

Set the valance on top of the angle brackets and screw the brackets to the boards with ⅝-inch screws.

One use for a wide wooden valance is to hide lightbulbs. Our valance project, starting on the previous page, could serve as this one does.

Rustic Boxed Beams with Corbels

Simple boxed beams supported at either end with carved corbels add decorative detail to a Folk, Tudor, or Rustic home. Both beams and corbels should be stained.

materials

- 2 × 4s, for nailers
- 1 × 4s or 1 × 6s, for sides
- 1 × 6s, for bottoms
- $7\frac{3}{8}$" × $3\frac{1}{4}$" × $3\frac{7}{8}$" corbels

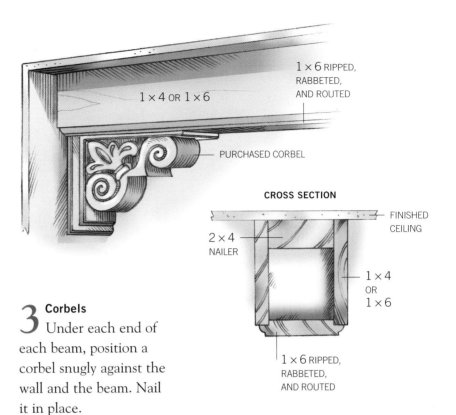

1 × 6 RIPPED, RABBETED, AND ROUTED

1 × 4 OR 1 × 6

PURCHASED CORBEL

CROSS SECTION

FINISHED CEILING

2 × 4 NAILER

1 × 4 OR 1 × 6

1 × 6 RIPPED, RABBETED, AND ROUTED

1 Create Layout, Install Nailers, and Install Sides

Follow steps 1 through 3 for the Arts and Crafts boxed-beam ceiling (pages 68–69), but space the beams 32 inches on center. For the sides of the beams, choose 1 × 4s or 1 × 6s, depending on the scale of the room and the effect you want.

2 Install Bottoms of Beams

For each beam, cut a 1 × 6 to the length of the beam. Rip the board to $4\frac{3}{4}$ inches. Rout both edges of one side with a $\frac{3}{8}$-inch bead bit (see illustration). Cut $\frac{1}{4}$-inch by $\frac{5}{8}$-inch rabbets on both edges of the other side. The rabbets should fit snugly over the bottoms of the beam sides. Glue the bottom to the sides and nail it into them.

3 Corbels

Under each end of each beam, position a corbel snugly against the wall and the beam. Nail it in place.

Carved corbels give just the right amount of ornamentation to a simple space.

japanese

Since the mid-1800s, Japanese architecture has inspired designers around the world. In America, the Arts and Crafts movement was greatly influenced by the Japanese style's simplicity, fine craftsmanship, and use of natural materials. Over the past 50 years, homeowners attracted to Japanese sensibility have continued to replicate or reinterpret Japanese architecture in America.

Japanese style is a concept rather than a form of decoration. In Japan, a house had to integrate the outdoors with the indoors to be considered a home. In fact, the ideogram for home is composed of *ka* for house and *tei* for garden. The effect was possible in traditional Japanese architecture because homes were built with post-and-beam construction, in which the walls did not support the roof. Therefore, entire walls could be composed of shoji screens. Made of wood and translucent paper, the screens could slide to the side or even be removed, so the interior space was completely open to the garden. To achieve a sense of tranquility, the Japanese style had no extraneous decoration. Structural elements were left exposed to display the perfect joinery that was a signature of this style, and simple wood trim showcased the natural beauty of the hardwoods used.

Today you can borrow many details of Japanese style for your own home. Most obviously, shoji

Shoji panels serve as doors and cover the walls, windows, and a ceiling light fixture; a shoji project is given on page 92. Note how the grid of the shojis is echoed in the square wooden floor panels.

screens can be used as window covers and as sliding doors between rooms or in front of closet openings. Above a door opening, you can add a transom made of flat wood paneling, thin bamboo slats, or translucent paper. For walls, you can use clear-stained hardwood panels or plaster painted flat white. A wood-trimmed niche offers a place to display Asian art or a flower arrangement.

A shoji-inspired sliding door is one-third wood, making it more durable for everyday use.

japanese projects

Most of the trim for a Japanese-style home should be made of a simple wood board, clear- or light-stained. The key is to use good wood, such as clear pine, birch, or fir. You'll also want to make your joints as clean as possible, to emulate the exquisite craftsmanship of Japanese joinery. Windows and doors can be trimmed in flat 1 × 4 casing, using butt joints at corners; the head casing can overhang the sides, as shown. The baseboard and cornice can be made with the same wood. One effective treatment is to extend a trim from the top of the door casings all the way around the room.

On the following page we show how to cover a window with a shoji screen. (You can also replace sliding closet doors with shoji panels, or install shojis on a track in front of sliding glass doors.) In addition, we have included a rectangular wall niche, which provides a simple space for a Japanese ceramic or an ikebana flower arrangement.

PROJECTS IN THE JAPANESE STYLE

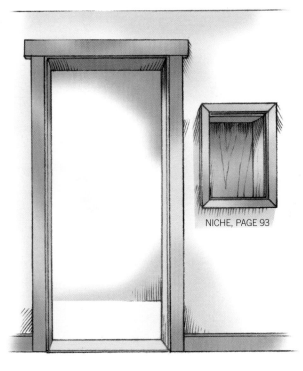

NICHE, PAGE 93

Shoji Window Screen

Shoji panels can be purchased as ready-made or custom items from specialty manufacturers (see Resources on page 126). Stock panels come in a range of sizes up to 48 inches wide and 96 inches tall. If your window requires a unique size (see step 1) or grid design, you may need to have a screen custom-made. Plan ahead, because custom panels may take weeks or months to fabricate. Our project calls for purchased pocket door hardware and track.

The window itself should be a simple slider or a double-hung window; if you have a casement window, the handle should not project beyond the wall. If you have wood-covered jambs, wood casings, or a wood stool, you may want to build out the track system so it is the same depth as the casing or stool (that is, if the casing is ¾ inch deep, put the top and bottom tracks on 1-by boards). If the window jambs are covered with wallboard, you can add the shoji tracks with no modifications.

When pulled aside, sliding shoji screens add visual interest to a room; when closed they provide privacy without blocking out light.

materials

- 2 × 2
- pocket door hardware and track
- 1 × 4, of same wood as shoji frame
- aluminum T molding
- 2 × 4, of same wood as shoji frame
- 2 prefabricated shoji screens, 1⅜ " thick (see step 1)

1 Measure Window and Buy Screens
Measure the height and width of the window opening. Divide the width in half and add 1 inch to determine the width of each shoji screen. Add ½ inch to the height to determine the height of the shoji screen. Purchase or order the screens.

2 Mark Level Line
Mark a level line 3½ inches above the top of the window opening.

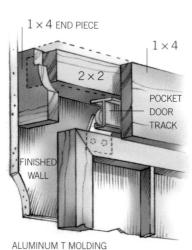

1 × 4 END PIECE

2 × 2

1 × 4

POCKET DOOR TRACK

FINISHED WALL

ALUMINUM T MOLDING

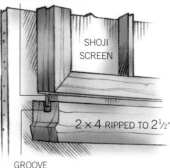

SHOJI SCREEN

2 × 4 RIPPED TO 2½"

GROOVE

3 Install Top Track
The track will be twice the width of the window, so when the screens are open, the whole window will be exposed to view. Double the measurement of the width of the window opening and add 2 inches. Cut a 2 × 2 to that length. Attach the pocket door track to the bottom of the 2 × 2 following the manufacturer's instructions. Center the 2 × 2 over the window along the level line you marked and nail it into the wall framing.

Cut a 1 × 4 to the same length plus 1½ inches. Center it with one edge flush with the top of the 2 × 2 (see illustration). Nail it into the 2 × 2.

4 Prepare Shoji Screen
Attach the pocket door hardware to the top of the shoji screen following the manufacturer's instructions. Cut a piece of aluminum T molding about an inch shorter than the width of the shoji screen. Center it on the bottom of the screen and screw it in place.

Wall Niche

See also illustration, page 91

materials

- 2 × 4s, for blocking
- 1 × 4s, for framing box
- ¼" plywood, for box back
- 1 × 2s, for face frame

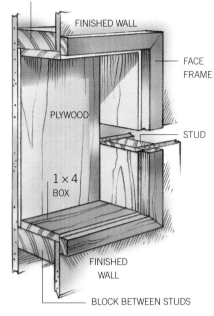

BLOCK BETWEEN STUDS

FINISHED WALL

FACE FRAME

PLYWOOD

STUD

1 × 4 BOX

FINISHED WALL

BLOCK BETWEEN STUDS

1 Create Opening
Locate the wall studs (see page 107). Mark the inside edges of the studs. Between them, mark level lines 24 inches apart for the top and bottom of the niche. Using a keyhole saw, cut out the wallboard between the lines.

Check for wiring and plumbing. If the area is clear, measure the distance between the studs (it should be approximately 14½ inches) and cut two 2 × 4s to that length for blocking. Slide the 2 × 4s into place behind the wallboard at the top and bottom of the opening, and toenail them into the studs on each side.

2 Make Box
Make the box by cutting two 1 × 4 boards 14¼ inches long and two boards 22⅜ inches long (check the exact dimensions of your opening; the box should be about ⅛ inch smaller in each direction so it will fit easily, but snugly, into the cavity). Butt the long boards against the short ones and nail them together; the box will be 14¼ inches wide and 23¾ inches high.

Cut the plywood 14¼ inches by 23¾ inches. Nail it with 1-inch nails to one side of the box, with the best side of the plywood facing the inside of the box.

3 Install Niche
Slide the box into the opening. The face of the box should be flush with the wallboard. Check the plumb and level of the box and shim it into place. Screw the box into the studs through the shims.

4 Add Face Frame
Measuring from the inside edge of the box, mark a ¼-inch reveal (see page 106). Measure from reveal to reveal for the length of the face frames. Cut and miter the framing pieces (see page 109) to fit around the box. Nail the frame into the front of the box and the wall studs with 2¼-inch finish nails.

5 Install Bottom Track
Cut a 2 × 4 to the same length as the 2 × 2 used for the top track and rip it to 2½ inches wide. Use a table saw or router equipped with a slot cutter of appropriate size to cut a groove centered on one narrow edge of the board. The groove should be as deep as the T molding. Sand both ends of the board. Position it under the bottom of the window opening, making sure it is level, and nail it into the wall framing.

6 Install Screen
Most track hardware comes with a pair of stops for the track. Push the stops to the outside edges of the top track. Tilt and slide the screens into position along the top and bottom tracks, then close up the ends of the housing for the top track: Measure from the wall to the back of the 1 × 4. Cut two pieces of 1 × 4 to that length. With the top edges flush and the front edges snug against the back of the 1 × 4, nail one cut 1 × 4 into each end of the 2 × 2.

Chapter 4

ON THE FOLLOWING pages we explain—and show—the techniques used in installing trim, from cutting molding to applying finishes. As you undertake the projects in Chapter 3,

trim techniques

you'll turn to these pages for guidance, but you can also use this information anytime you work with trim. ∽ Some of the techniques discussed here are very specific—the wall frame instructions on pages 118–120, for example—whereas others, such as the joinery explanations on pages 108–111, you'll use for many kinds of trim projects. Sequences such as those on casing (page 113) and returns (page 111) outline the best practices generally accepted by finish carpenters. ∽ For many trim projects, all you'll need are basic carpentry skills. The keys to success are selecting appropriate materials and tools, doing things in the right order, being meticulous about measuring, and knowing a few tricks of the trade, which we've included here. So no matter what kind of project you are working on, be sure to read pages 96–112 before starting. The basics discussed on these pages—everything from marking level lines (and fudging them when you have to) to finishing a cut end gracefully—are essential. Master them, and you'll have trim projects you can be proud of.

hand tools

Here's an overview of the hand tools you're most likely to want for a trim project.

Plumb bob This tool indicates perfect verticals. You'll use it to mark a spot on the floor directly below one on the ceiling (as in the column project on page 50). It is also an accurate way to mark a wall with a vertical line that's too long for your carpenter's level.

Chalk line Use this for marking guidelines on walls and plywood or other stock. Always check plumb and level lines with a spirit level.

Tape measure This is the basic tool for marking stock for crosscuts. Mark at the measurement you want and also mark the waste side of the cut (see page 103). Then mark the actual cutting line with a combination square or an angle square.

Angle square This one-piece tool also lets you mark 90- and 45-degree cuts and makes a good guide for a circular saw.

Sliding bevel This is an essential tool for measuring and duplicating angles. You loosen the setscrew, measure the angle, and tighten the screw, then use it to mark the angle where needed.

Framing square You can use this to check whether corners meet at a 90-degree angle and whether lengths of molding and wall panels are square to casings, or anytime horizontals must be square to verticals.

Combination square This adjustable tool lets you quickly mark 90- and 45-degree cuts, the most common cuts you'll make. It's also useful for measuring small pieces and marking a given distance from the edge of a board.

Protractor This is useful for transferring angles from the sliding bevel to the miter saw. Special adjustable protractors such as the one shown can measure angles like a sliding bevel, at the same time recording degrees for transfer to your miter saw.

Nail set Use this tool for countersinking finishing nails.

Nails Finishing nails are the fasteners of choice for trim work. You'll need 4-penny (4d), 6d, and 8d nails most often.

Hammer A standard 12- or 16-ounce nailing or framing hammer is fine for nailing moldings and driving your nail set. Be sure the hammer has a smooth face.

Screws For mounting backing blocks for crown molding, 3- or 4-inch wallboard screws are fast and strong. They're also useful for fastening heavy moldings—and those that must carry heavy weight—to framing. Counterbore for the heads, then fill and sand smooth.

Levels Use a carpenter's spirit level when laying out the job. One caution, however: Don't assume that everything that is perfectly level will look right. Always mark up the entire room, then step back and evaluate. Because the floor and ceiling may not be perfectly level, you may have to make things "half a bubble off" every now and then for your project to pass the eye test.

If you have large rooms with long walls, consider purchasing a laser level. It projects level lines on all four walls at once, greatly simplifying your work. You don't want the light shining in anyone's eyes, however, so follow all safety precautions noted in the instructions.

Clamps *Spring clamps,* C-clamps, *and* bar clamps *help you steady stock for cutting, drilling, and trimming, and they hold casings and other moldings in place at doorways and windows. Protect the clamped surfaces with small wood scraps.*

Rasps and files *Always handy, rasps and files are ideal for roughing out shapes, chamfering edges, and adjusting fit—of coped joints, for instance. A four-in-hand rasp, such as the one shown, is four tools in one: flat and half-round rasps, plus flat and half-round double-cut files.*

Utility knife *You'll need one of these for trimming and detail work. Change blades often: A sharp knife is better—and safer—than a dull one.*

Saws *A small* crosscut saw *or* backsaw *makes straight cuts and is also useful in simple miter boxes. Mark and cut on the good side of the wood.*

A hand miter box *with built-in, suspended* miter saw *makes extremely accurate straight and angled cuts. It's an excellent, economical tool for fine work and for doing a room or two, and it makes much less dust than its powered cousins (see page 98). However, it may not be practical for large projects or heavy moldings. Mark and cut on the good side of the wood.*

A coping saw *creates perfect inside corner joints (page 110). Support your work near the cutting line in a vise, or clamp it to your worktable. Because the saw cuts on the pull stroke, mark and cut on the good side of the wood, with the saw handle held beneath.*

Gap fillers *For painted trim, you'll need painter's caulk to fill minor gaps and wall patching compound for nail and screw holes. For clear-finished molding, use color-matched wood putty.*

Adhesives *Ordinary carpenter's glue works fine for assembling wood moldings—gluing joints, fastening lightweight stock to walls. Construction adhesive is better for heavy moldings or those that will bear a lot of weight.*

Block plane *Useful for trimming end grain, a block plane helps you make tight-fitting joints. The low-angle block plane works best but can be somewhat hard to find. Keep the blade sharp for fast, accurate results.*

power tools

Power tools greatly speed your work and, used properly, are often more accurate. Here's an overview of the ones to consider for a trim project.

Jigsaw Also called a saber saw, a jigsaw is best for cutting curves and making cutouts around obstacles such as electrical boxes and heating registers. Saws with orbital action work better in heavy stock than simpler models limited to straight up-and-down motion. A scrolling head is useful if you'll be doing a lot of tight curves. Because the blade cuts on the upstroke, mark and cut on the back side of the wood. If you must cut on the good side, use a very fine-tooth blade or a special downward-cutting blade.

Circular saw A circular saw is an ideal workhorse tool for straight cuts in plywood sheets and for rough-trimming boards. For crosscutting, an angle square makes a good guide. For ripping, use the saw's edge guide where possible; otherwise, clamp a straight board in place as a guide. Mark and cut on the back side of the wood.

Table saw This is an essential tool for making long dadoes and bevels, and for ripping lumber to special widths. However, if your trim project does not involve these tasks, you can do without a table saw. Cut with the good side up.

Power miter saw If you'll be installing more than a room's worth of molding, a power miter saw will repay you many times over in convenience and accuracy. For trim work, two types are best: the compound miter saw and the sliding compound miter saw. The former makes straight, angled, and beveled cuts—and can make straight or angled cuts with bevels at the same time. The latter makes the same cuts, but its sliding carriage allows you to draw the saw across wider work. For typical trim projects, a 10- or 12-inch compound miter saw is sufficient. With either power saw, you cut with the good side of the wood up.

Router This tool can be handy for rounding returns and is essential when you're making your own moldings. Used singly or in combination, the many bits available allow you to rout myriad profiles in board edges, creating custom casings and the like. This chore should not be undertaken lightly, however. Even if you mount your router in a router table, it's difficult to match the accuracy of commercially made moldings, whether they're stock or custom.

Sanders A random-orbit sander is the single most versatile power sander for general use. Most types have ventilation holes in the pads that remove sawdust as you work. For removing a good deal of material quickly, a belt sander is a good choice.

Power nailer If you have several rooms to do, consider buying or renting a nail gun or a pneumatic brad nailer. Accuracy is easy to achieve with these fast tools, and you never need a "third hand" the way you often do with a hammer and nails. Nail guns, which are common in general construction, are big and heavy. For a small trim project, or if you seldom do construction work, you may prefer a brad nailer such as the one shown. These tools can drive up to 2-inch, 18-gauge brads (big enough for average moldings) and are nearly as light as a hammer. Standard air-powered units require a compressor and hose. Gas-operated and electric guns allow you to work without these encumbrances.

Drill-driver A battery-operated cordless drill that also drives screws is the best tool for drilling pilot holes and driving screws. You'll appreciate its cord-free convenience. Most drill-drivers come with a charger and spare battery so that you can work without interruption. Ordinary twist bits are fine for most molding work. Brad-point bits are best for holes larger than ⅛ inch or so, because they cut more cleanly.

working safely

Although most trim work does not involve heavy construction, any do-it-yourself project does raise safety concerns. Following these guidelines will help you avoid injury.

When using a power tool for the first time, read the owner's manual and practice on some scrap wood. Always keep the tool unplugged if you will not be using it for an extended period, or when you are making an adjustment or changing a blade. To guard against deadly shocks, make sure that all power tools are connected to a GFCI-protected outlet. When you stop work, put power tools away so that children cannot get to them.

Wear safety goggles when using power tools. Use earplugs when operating any tool that is loud. Wear a dust mask when sanding.

When working in areas higher than what you can comfortably reach from the floor, you may want to use a scaffold; properly installed, it is the safest method. If you use a stepladder, be sure its load capacity is sufficient for the weight you need to put on it, including your own. The legs should be on a level surface. To work adjacent to where the ladder is placed, move the ladder rather than leaning out to the side. Avoid standing above the second rung from the top.

materials

Commercial moldings are made from a variety of materials. Here's a guide to your choices.

WOOD TRIM

Trim made of wood is generally stocked in both soft- and hard-woods. It is usually sold in lengths from 12 to 16 feet—often long enough to cover an entire wall. Paint-grade wood trim can be purchased preprimed; if pieces of wood have been finger-jointed together (this is called PFJ—primed finger joint—trim) to form longer lengths, make sure that the joints don't show through the primer.

You can buy wood trim off the shelf at a millwork supplier, lumberyard, or home improvement center, but availability varies from region to region. If your supplier doesn't stock the wood you want, you can request a special order, or you can investigate catalogs (see page 126) or the Internet. Special orders will include setup and tooling fees, which will add significantly to your cost. Most trim-work dealers can also do custom runs for you.

Or, if you're skillful with a router, you can make your own trim. Poplar and straight-grained pine are fine for moldings that will be painted. Make two or three shallow passes, working your way down to the final profile depth. For clear-finished trim work, it's

best to use hardwood. Rout cautiously, with several passes, because any errors will show. If you're making a lot of molding, a router table will speed your work and be safer and more accurate.

If you're working in the Arts and Crafts, Modern, or Japanese styles, you can do much of your trim work with flat stock. Good species for light-colored trim include pine, maple, birch, beech, and bamboo. For the stained trim used in Arts and Crafts schemes, Douglas fir or oak is suitable. When you are using flat boards for trim, look for S4S (surfaced four sides), which means that the boards have been smoothed on all faces and edges so that any exposed side looks attractive.

Most boards are sold in "nominal" sizes: The name by which they are known indicates their size before milling; actual sizes are smaller. Trim commonly uses "1-by" stock, which was about an inch thick before milling; the finished thickness is about $\frac{3}{4}$ inch. For Arts and Crafts schemes, you'll want $\frac{5}{4}$ and $\frac{4}{4}$ stock. These terms refer to the lumber thickness in quarter inches before milling. A $\frac{5}{4}$ board is about an inch thick; a $\frac{4}{4}$ is about $\frac{3}{4}$ inch thick.

Softwoods Most interior trim projects are done with stock softwood moldings. Clear, or stain-grade, moldings are made from single lengths of lumber without knots and are meant to be clear-finished (stained or unstained). Paint-grade moldings may have cosmetic flaws or be made up of many shorter pieces that are butt- or finger-jointed together. Pine, poplar, and bass-wood are all common species.

Hardwoods Hardwood moldings—oak, maple, and cherry, all more expensive than softwoods—evoke Old World craftsmanship. You'll probably need to visit a specialty dealer to find a wide variety.

Medium-density fiberboard (MDF) *This is a paint-grade trim that is less expensive than wood but when painted is difficult to distinguish from the real thing. Made by compressing wood fibers with resins, MDF trim has a smooth surface. Because it comes preprimed, it can usually be finished with one coat of paint, and it requires little or no sanding. It won't split when nailed and is more resistant to dings and dents than most softwoods. However, it's heavy, is best fastened with a nail gun, and will reflect every undulation in an uneven wall.*

Polyurethane trim *If your trim will be painted, high-density polyurethane is a lightweight, inexpensive alternative to wood. It comes in many patterns (including ornate classical profiles that are extremely expensive to duplicate in wood). The one-piece moldings, especially those that are joined together with corner blocks, are easy to install. Polyurethane can be cut and nailed into without cracking, splintering, or splitting. It requires no predrilling for nails or screws, no priming, and no sanding before painting. It won't rot, and it expands and contracts much less than wood when exposed to severe changes in temper-ature and humidity.*

Specialty pieces *Sometimes a project cries out for a special accent piece. Specialty pieces, both molded and hand carved, are available in hardwoods, softwoods, and composites to meet these needs. Specialty pieces are usually expensive, but then you don't need many to make a real difference in a room.*

Combination moldings *These moldings are first milled from poplar. Then a composite material, carrying highly figured "carved" designs, is bonded to them. The result is an elaborate piece of trim that would be prohibitively expensive to produce by other means. When painted (they cannot be clear-finished), these moldings lend great richness to a room.*

Custom moldings *Sometimes stock moldings don't quite create the look you're trying to achieve. Or you may need to match an older profile that is no longer made. For a setup charge, which includes grinding shaper knives for the profile you want, you can have a dealer make custom moldings. Although this is expensive for a single room, if you are doing a large project, the cost will be minimal when spread over the whole job.*

Flexible vinyl *As the name suggests, these moldings will follow a curving wall, creating an elegant effect. This is the only material that can make tight curves smoothly, as proved by the short length of baseboard shown here. Vinyl is cut and fastened just like wood; it is impervious to water.*

removing old trim

If you're replacing existing trim, it's out with the old before it's in with the new. In this case, you can pretty much just rip out the old trim, taking care not to damage walls in the process. If you want to reuse the old trim, however, perhaps after remodeling, you'll want to remove it carefully without damaging it. Here's how to proceed.

If paint is binding the molding to the wall, use a utility knife to score the paint along the edges of the molding. Then use a stiff putty knife to separate the molding slightly from the wall and create a space for pry bars. Slide the putty knife back and forth until you hit the finishing nails that hold the molding to the wall.

1 Insert a pry bar at one set of nails, and place a scrap of wood behind the bar to protect the wall. Pry gently outward to bow the molding away from the wall and loosen the nails. Move to the next set of nails and repeat the process until you've loosened the molding along its entire length.

2 Sometimes the nails won't loosen, and prying will cause the nails to pull through the molding. If the nails are stuck, use a nail set to drive them about three quarters of the way through the molding's thickness. You need not go all the way through.

3 Work with a pair of pry bars to remove the molding, leapfrogging the bars in turn to gradually ease the molding away from the wall without cracking or breaking it. With the molding off, use a hammer or pry bar to remove any nails that remain in the wall.

If you're planning to reinstall the molding in place, label each piece as you remove it. This will save much time and confusion later.

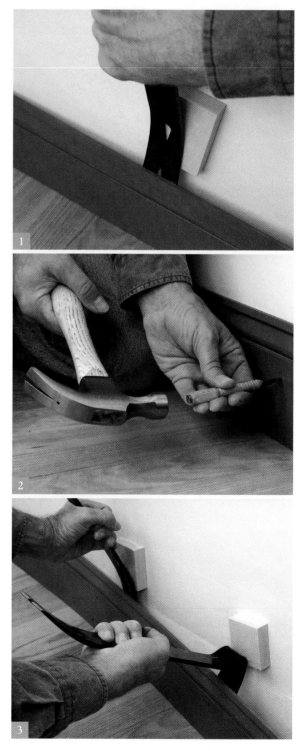

measuring accurately

Your measurements will be only as accurate as the tools you use. Test your tape measure against the metal rule of your combination square, checking that the sliding hook yields the same dimension whether it's hooked to the end of the rule or pushed flush against it. If the measurements aren't identical, bend the hook until the error is corrected. Check your 4-foot level, too. Lay out a level line on a wall, then flip the level end for end and read the line using the same vial. If there's even a slight discrepancy, plan on flipping the level back and forth as you work (a good idea, anyway). If it's way off, you may need a new tool.

When you're sure that your tools yield accurate measurements, you're ready to start. As you work, bear in mind that measurements can't be perfect even though the fit must often be. It's best to cut a trim piece a bit too long or too wide, then do trial fitting to get it just right. Pros nearly always use such "empirical" techniques.

Following are some methods of work that will ensure a quality job.

1 Once you've set the heights for your moldings, mark the locations for the entire suite of trim pieces on all walls of the room to see what the room will look like when you're done. If you feel it's not quite right, re-mark the room and evaluate it again; changing lines on the walls is far easier than removing trim once you've attached it.

To do the marking, avoid measuring repeatedly around the room; this invites errors. Instead, use a story pole—a piece of 1 × 2 or other light dimension lumber. Measure and mark the locations of the baseboard, chair rail, picture rail, and the like on the pole. (Crown molding is marked separately; see page 117.) Then, holding the story pole against the walls, transfer the markings, as shown. Snap chalk lines between marks, and you'll quickly get an idea of what your finished installation will look like. In the photo, the baseboard, chair rail, and picture rail have been laid out.

When you're marking trim to be cut, it's important to be consistent. Use a sharp pencil, and always be clear which side of a cutting line is the waste piece (pros mark it with an **X**, just to be sure). For critical measurements, mark trim with a utility knife or the scriber from a combination square. To avoid cumulative errors when laying out repeating elements, such as a series of wall frames, measure and mark each cut from a single starting point rather than from the previous mark. When cutting, cut just to the outside of your line, so that the line remains on the cut piece. When measuring, remember to allow for the saw's kerf (its thickness), which can be anything from a fine line to ⅛ inch or more.

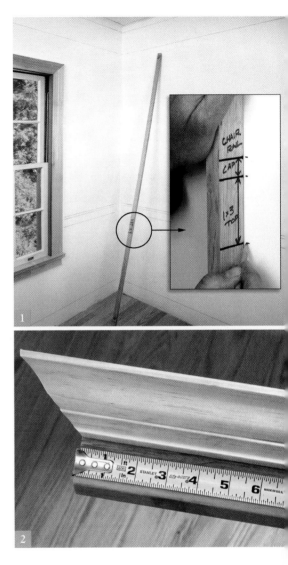

2 As you work you may find it awkward to mark some pieces for cutting: A tape measure simply can't be hooked to the end of mitered trim and other angular pieces. An old carpenter's trick helps here. Lay the piece to be cut on a square-cut 2 × 4, lining up the "unhookable" end with the end of the 2 × 4. Hook your tape to the 2 × 4 and run it alongside the molding piece; then mark the molding for cutting.

marking level lines

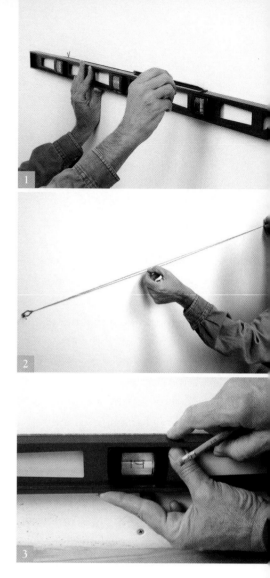

1 To mark a short level line, you can use a level to extend the line from a measured point.

2 Longer lines are best marked with a chalk line. Drive a brad at one measured point, then attach the chalk line, reel out the line to a second measured point, stretch the line tight, and snap the line on the wall. Then check the line with a level.

3 Once you've marked a line, use a 4-foot level to check it. Lightly mark a level line in any areas of concern and measure the difference between it and the original line. If a chalk line is "out" by only ¼ inch or so in 6 feet, you can probably go with it. Usually the eye will accept moldings that follow the floor line within these limits, especially baseboards. If the difference is more, use the level to re-mark the line, setting the line level or perhaps splitting the difference.

Remember that in molding work the goal is to produce a pleasing result, not a mathematically perfect one. It's a matter of eye. Your care and attention at this stage will be well rewarded down the line.

cutting and installing trim

Base and crown moldings and chair and picture rails usually continue all the way around a room. The order in which you install the molding pieces can make a difference in the effect they make, so it's best to plan your installation sequence carefully. Make a rough sketch of the room you're working on, then consider the following points.

For a basic rectangular room, start with the most visible moldings, the ones opposite the entry door. The first moldings will be square-cut where they meet adjoining walls. Once these starter pieces are installed, cut the adjoining pieces on either side, coping the corners (page 110). Cut their other ends square to butt against the adjacent walls. The final piece or pieces will be coped at both ends. On very long walls you may have to join shorter pieces with scarf joints (page 111). Cut them so that they point away from you when you enter the room.

Some rooms have a more irregular shape involving outside and inside corners. Outside corners project into the room; inside corners project away from the room. The former require mitered joints on trim (page 109); the latter require coped joints (page 110). To remember which way the miter goes, keep in mind that with an outside corner the cut trim pieces are longer on their outside surfaces—the ones facing the room. To cope an inside corner, remember that the first cut is an inside miter cut, yielding a piece that is longer on the inside surface—the one facing the wall. Start installing your trim with the irregular area that requires the miters, such as a bay, an alcove, or an ell (see illustrations).

When mounting mitered door and window casings, tack or clamp the pieces in place lightly at first. You'll probably have to make several adjustments to get everything lined up. Pros generally put up the side casings first, then trim and fit the head casing, but this can be challenging for an amateur. A better approach is to start with a single side casing, temporarily fastened at the reveal line (page 106), with the inner edge of the miter cut to touch the head-casing reveal line. Next, position the head casing, trimming it to fit against the mitered side casing on one side and the reveal line of the other side casing. Finally, cut and fit the other side casing, starting with it a little long and trimming the square-cut bottom until you get a good fit. Once everything fits properly, take the pieces down, add glue, and nail them in place. (For more about casings, see page 113.)

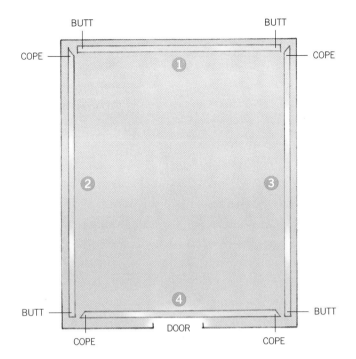

CUTTING SEQUENCE FOR CORNICE MOLDING, BASIC RECTANGULAR ROOM

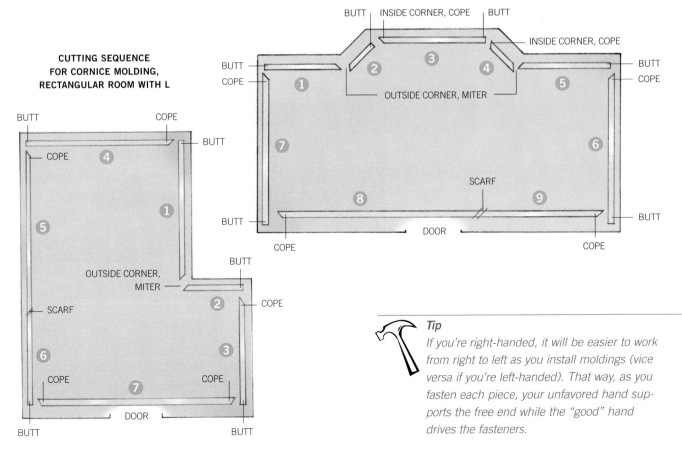

CUTTING SEQUENCE FOR CORNICE MOLDING, RECTANGULAR ROOM WITH BAY WINDOW

CUTTING SEQUENCE FOR CORNICE MOLDING, RECTANGULAR ROOM WITH L

Tip

If you're right-handed, it will be easier to work from right to left as you install moldings (vice versa if you're left-handed). That way, as you fasten each piece, your unfavored hand supports the free end while the "good" hand drives the fasteners.

creating a reveal

When door and window jambs are installed, there is an unsightly gap between the wall material and the jamb stock. Casing covers that gap (page 113). It's customary to install casing so that it overlaps all but a little of the jamb—⅛ to ¼ inch. This small amount of casing left revealed is called just that—a reveal. The term *reveal* is also used to describe any situation in which one material partially covers another, leaving some exposed. A reveal creates an elegant transition between one material and another. And it's easier to have a reveal than to try to align perfectly the casing and the jamb.

Although it may seem like a small thing, creating good reveals makes a huge difference in your finished work. When moldings meet, create reveals carefully. Well-proportioned reveals produce a delightfully complex interplay of light and shadow. As with so many things, the beauty is in the details. Here are some aspects to plan for.

1 On the inside edges of the casing, a fraction of an inch of jamb stock shows—this is the basic reveal. It should be at least ⅛ inch, but the best effect results from making it about the same as the thickness of the casing as it meets the jamb stock. A thicker casing calls for a wider reveal, although ¼ inch or so is probably the upper limit. The reveal shown here is about 3⁄16 inch wide, matching the thickness of the inside edge of the tapered casing.

2 There's more to reveals than just jambs and casings. This Neoclassical doorway features an elaborate head casing with two separate reveals. The first is at the side and top of the jamb. The second is on the frieze board, which sits on the top piece of door casing. The inset on its side equals the amount it is set back from the casing in front, so the frieze board is recessed from the door casing by equal amounts—reveals—on all sides. Following this general principle when possible—keeping side reveals equal to front reveals—will make your molding work look professional.

3 Plinth-and-corner-block casings, such as this Victorian example, also involve multiple reveals. Here, the plinth block is set to create a ⅛-inch reveal on the jamb. Then reeded casing is centered on the plinth, creating a wider reveal on the jamb. Where the casing meets the plinth block, the plinth-block thickness and width create equal side and front reveals. At the top, the side and top casings die into the corner block, which, like the plinth below, is both wide enough and thick enough to create equal reveals at the side and to the front. Note that the jamb reveal continues across the top of the door.

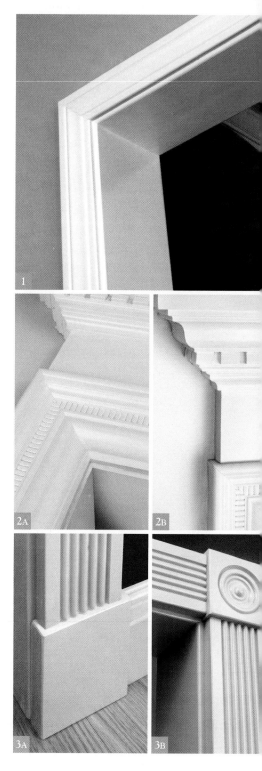

dealing with irregularities

In the real world, walls, ceilings, and floors are never truly flat or level, and rarely if ever do two of them meet at a perfect 90-degree angle. For outside-corner mitered joints (page 109) and miters on flat surfaces such as wall frames (page 118), always measure the actual angle. If it's "out" by more than 3 degrees or so, adjust your saw to bisect the angle. Trim for smaller variances with a plane, rasp, and sandpaper. Utilize the following time-tested methods to camouflage other irregularities.

IRREGULAR WALLS

Walls may have bumps and hollows that moldings cannot—and should not—follow. Because the eye more readily accepts a molding that's straight than one that curves even a little, it's best to fasten the molding to the high points and fill in the low ones. Use painter's

caulk to fill gaps up to ⅛ inch or so; use thin wood shims to fill in larger gaps, gluing or nailing the shims in place and caulking around them. With a utility knife or trim saw, cut shims flush with the molding edge.

UNEVEN CEILINGS

1 When a molding is set against a ceiling, it will be only as level as the ceiling itself. Use a 4-foot level to check crown moldings. In this photograph, the bubble is slightly off center. This is a small enough discrepancy to overlook: Even ¼ inch in 6 feet or so is okay. If the discrepancy is greater, level the molding, tack it in place, and see how it looks. Adjust as needed: You may wind up splitting the difference. When you're satisfied, fasten the molding in place and caulk any gaps.

2 Sprung crown molding should follow the layout line marked on the ceiling (page 117); the line marked on the wall is for reference only. Once you've fastened the molding to the ceiling, you may see gaps between its lower edge and the wall. Small gaps can be filled with caulk or wall patching compound. Shim and caulk gaps greater than ⅛ inch. Predrill and nail through the shim; cut off the excess shim with a utility knife or trim saw, and caulk.

Tip
Sometimes, especially in older homes, ceiling moldings actually look better when they are held ¼ inch or so away from an irregular ceiling and left uncaulked. Try it out.

UNEVEN FLOORS

You'll want to attach baseboard at or near level to serve as an accurate baseline for moldings farther up. If the floor is out of level, a tapering gap appears between the baseboard and the floor. Shoe molding will cover such a gap. Fasten the baseboard first, then nail the shoe molding in place, flexing it to follow any large undulations in the floor. Caulk any minor gaps that remain.

making secure attachments

For stability, all moldings—especially weight-bearing moldings such as picture rails and plate rails—should be attached to the wall studs. Finding studs can be a little tricky. Standard methods include tapping on the wall with your knuckle (the sound changes) and using a stud finder (the needle shows you). Or you can check the area around wall sockets and switches, which are nearly always attached to studs. A surefire way is to drive small nails or drill ⅛-inch holes every inch or so along the wall in the area to be covered by the molding until you hit a stud (solid hammering and sawdust are the giveaways).

Once you've found a stud, the others should be 16 inches away on center on either side. After locating and marking the wall studs along the length of molding you're installing, mark a level line (page 104) and position the molding against it.

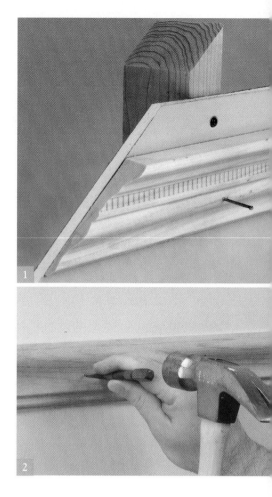

1 To attach the molding, use finishing nails and follow this rule of thumb: The nail should be long enough to penetrate the stud to a depth equal to two times the combined thickness of the trim material and the wall material. Thus, for ½-inch-thick molding and ½-inch wallboard, you will need 3-inch (10-penny) nails—1 inch to go through the molding and wallboard and 2 inches to penetrate the stud. Sixteen-penny (16d) nails are usually sufficient for thick moldings and for those that must carry a lot of weight. Use construction adhesive with the nails to add strength. For the best appearance (and to prevent splitting, especially at the ends of molding pieces), drill pilot holes, making them slightly smaller than the diameter of the nail.

2 Drive finishing nails at least ½ inch from the top and bottom edges of the molding, into surfaces on the molding that will be easy to fill with wall patching compound. Hammer the nails to within ¾ inch of the surface, then use a nail set to drive them below the surface. Finish with wall patching compound (if trim will be painted) or wood putty (if it will be clear-finished).

creating joints

Joinery lies at the heart of trim work. From the choice of the most suitable joint to its execution, good joints can make or break the effect. Often, simplest is best, together with a few tricks of the trade, as the following guidelines explain.

BUTT JOINTS

The simplest joint is the butt joint, where one piece is just positioned flat against the other. Painter's caulk is applied to seal the edges of the molding to the wall. Use a butt joint where two pieces of square-profile molding meet at an inside corner; where side casings meet the window stool, plinth blocks, or floor; and where a piece of thin molding joins a thicker piece. Avoid using a butt joint at an outside corner: The exposed end grain will be difficult to fill and then cover with paint, and if the trim is to be stained, the end will simply look unattractive.

A good butt joint must be gap-free, with a near-invisible line where the two pieces come together. Caulk may fill a tiny gap but may open up in time, so it's best to make the joint correctly in the first place. Test-fit the pieces and, if necessary, back-cut the mating piece with a saw or block plane to achieve a tight fit on the face.

MITERED JOINTS

Two pieces of trim meeting at an angle form a mitered joint. The most common is the 45-degree cut used to turn a 90-degree corner. Miters can be cut across the face of the molding—as shown below for a window casing (page 113)—or across its thickness, as for a return (page 111) or a scarf joint (page 111). Compound miters, mostly confined to crown moldings, are cut across both the face and the thickness (page 117).

An outside corner, which is formed by a projection into a room, requires outside miters in crown molding, chair and picture rail, and baseboard. An inside corner will join seamlessly when you cope the joints; start the joint with a miter cut (page 109). Flat miters, which are used at the corners on many door and window casings (page 113) and in wall frames (page 118), are like the joints in a picture frame. If the wall is irregular, a flat miter may need to be back-cut or otherwise trimmed to allow the joint to close without a gap.

For accuracy, the mating pieces must be cut at exactly the same angle, bisecting the total angle to be framed. For angles that total 90 degrees, or a little more or less, you can generally rely on your miter saw's angle guides for cutting, then trim to make minor adjustments. For other angles, measure with a sliding bevel and divide the total angle in half with a protractor. Set your miter saw to this angle, then cut and test-fit the pieces. Trim, if necessary, with the saw or a block plane. You can back-cut slightly if needed to produce a tight face to the joint.

Test-fit the pieces, predrill, then nail them in place, putting one nail through from an edge to help keep the joint together. In the photo, this "clinching" nail is on the left edge of the casing. To avoid splitting, keep the nails away from the ends of the joints by ¾ inch or so.

Tip

Always place the molding on the saw table in the same position that it will be on the wall, ceiling, or whatever you're attaching it to. To stay oriented, just think of the saw table as the surface the molding will be attached to (see page 117).

COPED JOINTS

Coped joints are asymmetrical: One side is butted into the corner, then the other side is cut to fit against the profile of the butted piece.

It's best to use a coped joint at inside corners for baseboards, chair and picture rails, and crown moldings. It's the only way to easily create a gap-free joint with complex moldings, a joint that will remain tight even when walls are out of square, and through seasonal changes that can open up other joints. Although coped joints may seem complicated at first, they actually save labor. Once you've cut a few, you'll find that they're easy to make—much easier than trying to caulk inaccurate miters at inside corners.

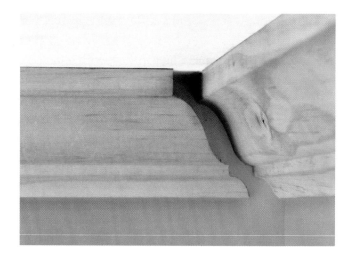

1 First, miter-cut the molding at 45 degrees, with the back edge longer than the front. Now you will cope the back side: Trim away the excess to create a mirror image of the molding's contours. The front edge of the cut, which follows the molding's profile (this is called revealing the profile), is the cutting line. Rubbing a pencil over this edge will make the cutting line more visible.

2 Hold the coping saw above the molding with the blade perpendicular to it, as if you were going to square-cut the end. Cut from top to bottom, following the curves of the front edge. In the middle of the cut, angle the blade so that it back-cuts, then return the blade to the perpendicular to finish the cut. Test-fit the joint: It will probably require some adjustment. With small rasps or files, carefully adjust the cut edge (thin edges can break easily) until you get a good, tight fit. Nail the molding to the wall, and caulk any gaps.

SCARF JOINTS

When a wall is too long to be spanned by a single piece of molding, you'll need to join separate pieces. Avoid just butting them together: The resulting line will show through even the best sanding and painting job. Instead, use a scarf joint, centering it over a stud if possible.

Plan the joint to point away from the most likely angle of view; this will help make it hard to spot. First, cut the mating pieces at opposing angles. A 30-degree angle is best if your saw can manage it; if not, you can cut the pieces at 45 degrees. Sand lightly to remove any roughness left by the blade. Position the joint carefully along a marked line on the wall, supporting it with a tacked-on 1 × 4 or other light, straight board. Fasten the joint with glue and nails, and give it a light final sanding. Once it's finished, the joint should be nearly invisible.

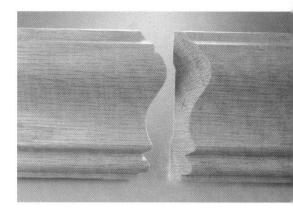

creating returns

1 A return is a treatment for a cut end of molding that allows the profile to continue, or return, to the wall. Returning provides a graceful touch that can make moldings really shine. Simple moldings—rectangular stock, half-rounds, quarter-rounds, and the like—can be bevel-cut, filled, and painted, as illustrated in the higher of the moldings shown here. To create a beveled return, simply cut the molding at an angle, but you don't need to automatically go for 45 degrees. Instead, experiment with steeper and shallower angles, checking them against the play of light and shadow in the room.

2 More complex moldings require coped or mitered returns. The apron on the window shown here has a coped return. These are the most difficult returns to make; miters (see below) are the returns of choice unless you're very comfortable with coping. To make the coped return, first cut the molding square. Then stand a scrap of the same molding at a right angle on the face of the molding, near the cut edge. Trace the profile on the piece, and cut it out with a coping saw.

3 Miters are easy to cut with a miter saw. Finishing a mitered return is also easy, as it covers the end grain. Because they turn the molding profile 90 degrees, mitered returns create a pleasing interplay of pattern, light, and shadow on the wall. To create a mitered return, first measure for the overall length of molding and cut a piece several inches longer than needed. Next, cut the small piece that will be the return: Cut a 45-degree inside miter at one end of the long molding piece (see photo, page 112), aligning the molding so that the saw just intersects its back corner. This gives you the small, triangular return piece. Now adjust the miter saw 45 degrees the other way (or flip the molding over) and make the mating miter cut at the end of the molding. If you're working with dentil molding or stock with an incised pattern, this method has the added advantage of carrying the pattern of the face piece onto the return piece nearly seamlessly.

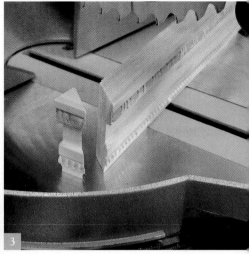

4 You can glue the pieces together on a worktable; when the glue is dry, sand the back flat. This two-step operation gives you a very accurate piece of molding. Alternatively, you can mount the long piece on the wall, then glue in the return piece, sanding if necessary to get a good fit.

trimming door and window openings

Casing is a general term for molding used to trim door and window openings. It works much like a picture frame to define and set off an opening in a wall. And, as a practical matter, it serves to cover the gap between a jamb and the adjacent wall surface. Casing is flat in back but varies widely (even wildly) on its face. From flat Arts and Crafts moldings through simple, modern shapes to elegant Colonial and elaborate Neoclassical styles, casing comes in a huge variety of profiles. Here's how to use it.

To begin, measure all the windows to determine how much molding you'll need, then add 10 to 15 percent for insurance.

Start work on the largest windows first, progressing to the smallest. That way, if you cut a piece too short, you may be able to use it on another window.

Next, be sure that the window jambs are flush with the surrounding wall; often they are not. If the jambs project past the wall surface, plane them until they are flush. If they fall short, glue filler pieces to the jamb stock. The filler pieces should be thick enough that the jambs will stand a little "proud" of the wall; when the glue is dry, plane them flush. To get the best fit for the casings, you can plane a slight back bevel on the wall side of the jambs.

CASING JOINTS

When you're installing casing on doors and windows, joinery is usually easy, involving only mitered and butt joints (pages 108–109). However, measuring is critical. It's easy to waste many feet of stock if you cut too short, so plan to cut a little long, then trim to fit. Casing is usually "held in" (which means set back) from the edge of the jamb by at least ⅛ inch, which creates a reveal (page 106). When you install any casing, first mark the reveal lines with a combination square, then measure for the casing pieces.

1 A typical casing scheme pairs mitered joints (page 109) at the top with butt joints (page 108) at the bottom. This casing scheme is commonly used for windows that have an apron and stool and, as shown here, for doorways. It's easiest for non-professionals to cut and fit one side, then the top, then the other side, cutting the last piece a little long and trimming the bottom joint to fit (page 105).

2 Use picture-frame casing to trim out windows that lack an apron and stool. To make sure the frame is square, the sides must be equal, the top and bottom must be equal, and the mitered cuts must be exactly 45 degrees. You may find that the opening you are casing isn't exactly square, in which case the reveals may taper instead of running straight. If possible, shim or reinstall the jambs to square them up. Otherwise, adjust your mitered joints by eye for the best appearance.

3 Arts and Crafts casing schemes are easy to install because they use butt joints at all intersections, including where the casing meets the floor or window stool. The casing pieces are made from flat stock, frequently a ⅝ piece for the head casing and ¼ pieces for the sides (page 100). This creates a front reveal where the sides die into the head. Ideally, you should create a side reveal equal to the front reveal (about ¼ inch when using ⅝ and ¼ stock). The ends of head casings are usually square-cut, but in practice, as in this example, builders may exercise artistic license. Cut and install the side pieces first, then the head casing.

CORNER BLOCKS AND PLINTHS

Most often used in the Neoclassical and Victorian styles, corner blocks and plinths lend elegance to doorways and windows. The simple butt joint makes this casing style particularly good for disguising an uneven wall (as opposed to a miter, which must lie flat).

1 Corner blocks and plinths should be selected in, or trimmed to, dimensions that create equal reveals to the front and sides of the casing (page 106). In addition, the height of the plinth should be at least equal to the height of the baseboard plus the amount of the reveal where the baseboard meets the plinth. Chamfer the plinths and corner blocks before installing them. The joinery is easy, although accurate measurements are critical. Starting at the bottom, position the plinth to create a ⅛-inch reveal to the jamb. Then cut the side casings to a length that will create an equal reveal on the head jamb. Install the side casings and corner blocks, then cut and fit the head casing.

2 If you are running a separate milled piece on top of the baseboard, use the same molding around the top of the plinth. If you're using a one-piece molded baseboard, as shown here, look for a harmonious molding to run atop the plinth.

creating window stools and aprons

A trim project may involve installing a new window stool (the horizontal "table" that sits on the sill and extends into the room) and a new apron (the molding that supports the stool from beneath and is attached to the wall). Note: The stool is often called the sill. Architecturally speaking, however, the sill is the horizontal piece that extends from the outside of the house to the inside, usually slanted to shed rain. The stool covers the sill on the inside. In new construction, you'll start from scratch, adding stool, apron, and casing to trim out a window. If you're replacing trim, you may be able to leave the stool in place, changing only the apron and casing.

The stool is a single piece cut to fit within the window opening, with "horns" that run in front of and beneath the window casing and beyond it a distance equal to the thickness of the casing. The stool can be made of molded ¹¹⁄₁₆-inch stool stock, or you can use clear, straight-grained lumber, routing or chamfering the edges to suit. The stool is installed before the casings.

1 To mark the width of the stool, hold a piece of side casing against the reveal line on one side of the window and mark its outside edge on the wall; repeat for the other side. Now measure the thickness of the casing stock and mark that amount outside the casing lines. Measure between these outer marks and cut the stool to this measurement. If you'll be creating a return in the stool, which is recommended for the best appearance (for more on returns, see page 111), cut the ends of the stool at 45 degrees (see photo 2). Alternatively, you can shape the ends of the stool to match its front profile, although this will expose end grain.

Next, measure from the sash to the edge of the sill. To this number add twice the thickness of the casing, then subtract $\frac{1}{16}$ inch: This is the depth measurement for the stool. Rip the stool to this size.

Now cut the notches that create the horns of the stool. First, mark the center of the sill and of the stool. Press the stool against the jambs, lining up the two marks, so that the stool is centered in the window opening. Mark the points where the side jambs intersect the stool. With a square, extend these marks across the stool. For the depth of the notch, measure from the sash to the edge of the sill at each side. Subtract $\frac{1}{16}$ inch and mark this amount on the stool at the side-jamb marks. Extend this measurement to the ends of the stool, then cut out the notches with

a jigsaw or coping saw. Check the fit against the wall and for clearance to the sash; fine-tune, if necessary, with a rasp and sandpaper.

Tack the stool to the sill with 18-gauge or 4d finishing nails, 10 inches on center, predrilling for the nails. Use glue for extra holding power, and drive the nails at a slight angle into the sill.

2 To finish the stool, cut and fit a return piece at each end. Fasten the return pieces with glue.

3 With the stool in place, cut and attach the casings (page 112). Next, cut and attach the apron. The edges of the apron should align with the casing edges, as shown. Measure between the casing lines you made earlier and cut the apron stock to this measurement. The apron's edge profile should match its face. Create the edge by mitering and returning the apron as you did the stool, or by coping its ends (page 110). Attach the apron to the stool and wall with glue, and nail it into the framing with 6d finishing nails. When the glue is dry, predrill, then drive 4d finishing nails through the stool into the apron every 10 inches.

To complete the assembly, countersink all nails. If you're painting, fill the nail holes with wall patching compound. If you're using a clear finish or stain, apply the complete finish first (see page 124), then use a matching putty stick to fill the nail holes.

installing horizontal moldings

Horizontal, wall-mounted moldings include baseboard at floor level, chair rail about a third of the way up the wall, plate rail still higher, and—making a return after decades of absence— picture rail above that. Flat-backed molding used as cornice, at the top of the wall, is also in this category. All these trims are installed in the same way.

All horizontal moldings should be fastened to the studs (page 108). This is especially important for weight-bearing moldings such as plate and picture rails, but it's good practice in general for making sure that moldings stay put. Mark the wall framing, and use at least 8d finishing nails for thin moldings, and up to 16d for heavy ones. Tall baseboards and other large trim should be nailed both top and bottom, to prevent the wood from cupping.

It's best to apply baseboard over a finished floor if possible. Otherwise, a floor-finishing sander will almost certainly damage the baseboard.

1 In most rooms, one kind of trim meets another; for instance, a baseboard will run into a door casing. One aspect of planning a suite of trim is making sure that these meetings are attractive. First, consider scale and proportion (page 10). Then, consider the type of joinery, or transition, to use at the meeting point (pages 104–105). For flat moldings or thick casings, simple butt joints often suffice. At the base of door and window casings, plinths give a substantial surface for baseboards to butt into (page 114). A chair rail that is deeper than the casings it meets looks good when returned onto the casings; see page 111 for return options. On this kitchen island, crown and baseboard moldings weave artfully around pilasters,

which gives visual support to a granite countertop. The baseboards become, in effect, plinths to carry the pilasters. Above and below, mitered returns (page 111) and well-proportioned reveals (page 106) create a sophisticated, finished look.

2 Moldings often encounter obstacles—heat registers, cold-air returns, electrical outlets, and more. In some cases you may cut a hole in the molding, but more often you'll want to run the molding around the obstacle. This opens up creative possibilities. Tall baseboards should be ripped to decrease their height so that the resulting frame around the obstacle won't be too large, as shown here. Conversely, when a molding meets a wall switch or outlet, you can often double the width of the molding, effectively creating an "island" for the switch or outlet to sit upon.

installing crown molding

O f all the interior trim options available, crown molding makes the greatest impact in an otherwise plain room. Gracefully bridging the transition between walls and ceiling, it provides an eye-pleasing line that delineates the space.

1 To mark for crown molding, use a 3- to 4-foot length of the molding itself as a guide rather than a ruler or tape measure. Holding the molding in place, mark the ceiling first, then the wall line.

2 Cutting crown molding can be a bit confusing. As you move from ceiling to saw, it's easy to lose track of what cut goes where. Here's an easy way to stay oriented: Think of the ceiling as a picture in a frame, with the crown molding acting as the frame. When you're cutting, the surface of the saw table becomes the "picture," and the saw fence the "wall." This means that you will make all cuts with the moldings upside down, as shown in the photo. Keep this in mind, and you won't be confused about which way to place the stock on the saw. You should cope joints wherever possible, so inside-corner junctions will have a square cut on one piece and an inside miter on its mate, which is then coped (page 110). Outside corners, if you have any, require outside miters on both mating pieces (page 109). Fine-tune the fit with a block plane, rasp, and sandpaper.

Install crown molding with nails and glue, predrilling and driving the nails into the wall framing wherever possible. With large, heavy crowns, you may want to use backing blocks. Cut triangular blocks from 2-by stock of sufficient width to fill in the angled back of the crown. Screw the blocks to the wall framing with 3-inch wallboard screws. Nail the crown molding to the blocks.

When you fasten crown molding, nail it to the ceiling first, then the wall. This ensures a true line at the ceiling, where the eye most needs to see it. Any gaps that may appear in the wall line due to irregularities in the wall surface are usually easy to handle (page 107). If the ceiling is uneven, test-fit with the molding resting on the bumps, shimming and caulking in the hollows. This will usually look fine. In extreme cases, you may want to run the molding ¼ inch below the ceiling and leave it uncaulked.

Tip

With a compound miter saw, you can cut crown molding flat on the saw table, often the most accurate way to go. Most crown molding "springs" at either a 45- or 52-degree angle to the wall. For 90-degree corners with 45-degree molding, set the saw's left tilt at 30 degrees and the miter angle at 35.3 degrees. For 90-degree corners with 52-degree molding, set the left tilt at 33.9 degrees and the miter angle at 31.6 degrees. Make test cuts until you get satisfactory results.

wall treatments

CREATING WALL FRAMES

Wall frames are just raised trim work—usually rectangles—mounted directly on the wall. They are most commonly used below (sometimes above) a chair rail to break up long expanses into more pleasing, rhythmic units. Simple in concept, subtle in execution, they dress up a room like nothing else, and they're usually easier and less expensive to install than wainscoting. They may be stained or painted, either matching the wall or contrasting with it; sometimes they are painted two or three colors.

Wall frames are always part of a molding suite, so proportions are important. The base molding should be taller than the chair rail; crowns and casings should be proportioned to the base molding; and the wall frame stock should be the smallest. Band molding and wall molding are the usual choices, but other types may work.

SIZING THE FRAMES One way of making attractive wall frames is to employ the Golden Rectangle rule of proportions. The rule states that the most pleasing rectangle has sides with a ratio of approximately 1:1.618. For practical purposes, a rectangle whose sides have a ratio of 5:8 is about right.

Try to adhere to the Golden Rectangle rule for the basic frames that repeat around the room, realizing that there will be exceptions with individual frames.

1 In rooms with a chair rail at 36 inches or lower, and in rooms with an 8-foot-high ceiling, horizontal frames usually look best. When the chair rail is at 60 inches, or the ceiling is 9 feet or higher, vertical frames are better. All the frames don't have to be of equal size. If there are many irregularities—doors, a fireplace—to work around, it may not be possible to make frames equal. In addition, a combination of sizes may be more attractive—see the illustrations opposite.

To begin, mark the walls for all your frames. You'll want to see each frame width and height (outside to outside of the molding) on the wall before you start cutting wood.

You'll make your plan based on a frame module—one frame plus one vertical margin; at the end of

PLANNING WALL FRAMES

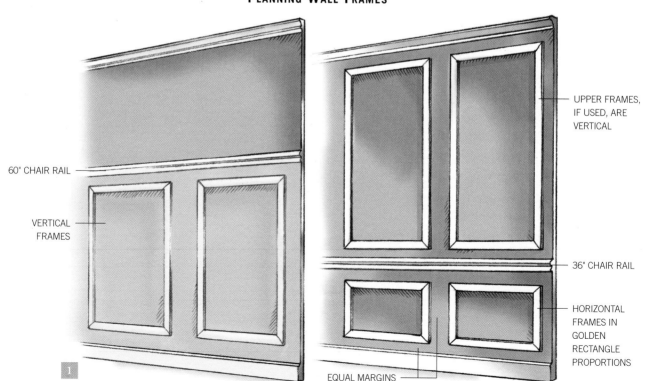

60" CHAIR RAIL

VERTICAL FRAMES

UPPER FRAMES, IF USED, ARE VERTICAL

36" CHAIR RAIL

HORIZONTAL FRAMES IN GOLDEN RECTANGLE PROPORTIONS

EQUAL MARGINS

1

the wall, add one more vertical margin. The margins should be uniform—between 2½ and 3 inches wide—on all sides, although sometimes making the bottom a little deeper than the other three sides looks good.

Measure the length of the walls. Make a tentative decision on the size of the margins. Now figure the number of frame modules you'll need per wall, and the width of the frames. This is a trial and error process that will go best if you use a calculator. Apply the formula at right, starting with an estimate of the number of frame modules that will fit on the wall and refining the number as the formula yields results. Use inches for all measurements.

Calculating Frame Size

$$\text{Frame width} = \frac{\text{wall length} - X}{\text{number of frame modules}}$$

X = width of the vertical margin, times the number of frame modules, plus one more vertical margin

The frame height is the distance from chair rail to baseboard minus two horizontal margins. Check the ratio of frame width to height against the Golden Rectangle (divide the long dimension by the short one). Continue adjusting the number of frame modules and the size of the vertical margins until you get closest to an ideal rectangle (1:1.618).

Example: *The wall is 16 feet long, or 192 inches. You choose 3-inch margins. The chair rail is at 36 inches and there's a 4-inch baseboard. Estimate 4 modules on the wall. To get* X: *3 (inches, vertical margin)* × *4 (modules) = 12; add 3 (one more vertical margin) = 15. 192 –15 = 177. 177 ÷ 4 = frame width of 44.25 inches. For height, 36 (chair rail height) – 4 (baseboard) = 32 inches – 2 horizontal margins of 3 inches each = 26 inches. Dividing the long dimension by the short one (44.25 ÷ 26), we get 1.7, not too far from the Golden Rectangle figure of 1.618. If you want to get closer to the ideal proportions, you might enlarge the vertical margins at the ends of the wall.*

VARYING WALL FRAMES

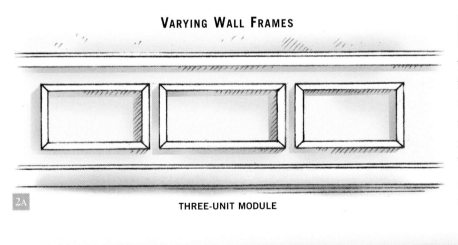

2A

THREE-UNIT MODULE

2 Frames need not be equal in width. You can make your module a group of three frames, with the middle one wider than those flanking it. Or work with a group of five frames, alternating narrow and wide ones. Try to make a standard frame (or frames) in the group comply with the Golden Rectangle.

2B

FIVE-UNIT MODULE

3 Obstacles create exceptions. Doors and windows often dictate special dimensions for frames. If a door or window is near an adjoining wall, you may not want to use a frame at all in the fragment of space. Wall frames under windows should always line up with the window casings. Thus, the vertical margins under windows will be unique and may vary from those on the rest of the wall, especially in the case of a bay window. Frame height will also vary under windows and other obstacles. If you encounter a wall socket or switch, you can mount it on a block of wood into which the wall frame can butt.

WORKING AROUND OBSTACLES

FRAME ALIGNS WITH CASINGS

OUTLET SET ON BLOCK

3

NARROW SPACE HAS NO FRAME

4 For strength and accuracy, it's best to assemble each frame on a plywood jig. You can make the jig from two pieces of ½-inch plywood, one for the base and one for the alignment guide. The base should be about 2 feet square. The alignment guide should fit within the smallest wall frame you're making, with two "factory edges" forming a 90-degree corner, which you'll use to align your frame corners. Screw the guide to the base a couple of inches inside its edges.

To assemble a frame, first miter-cut the frame pieces. Assemble one long and one short side on the jig, using glue. For fasteners, use a pneumatic brad nailer, or a hammer with nails or brads; if you're nailing, predrill for the fasteners. Set this part of the

frame aside to dry, meanwhile assembling the other two pieces. When these subassemblies are dry, glue and nail them together, using the jig as a guide.

INSTALLING FRAMES Key to the effect of wall frames is to install them uniformly below the chair rail and from one another, with vertical sides truly vertical. To begin, cut a spacer block equal to the margin width and at least 6 inches long. Place the block against the lower edge of the chair rail and hold a pencil at the lower edge of the block. Slide the spacer and pencil along the chair rail, marking a line to indicate the top edges of the frames. Measure and mark the top corners of each frame along this line.

If you're nailing by hand, predrill the frames for 6d finishing nails and insert the nails. (If you're using a pneumatic brad nailer, you can skip the predrilling.) Install one frame at a time. First, apply dots of construction adhesive to the back side. Then hold the spacer block against the chair rail, position the frame against the block, align the frame with its corner marks, and nail just the top in place. (Don't skip the adhesive: The nails will rarely hit a framing member, so the adhesive does most of the holding.) Next, plumb the sides with a short level, fasten them, then fasten the bottom. To complete the frame, set the nails and apply wall patching compound or putty. Caulk around the inside and outside of the frame.

CREATING WAINSCOTING

Wainscoting—boards or panels that run partway up the wall—is a signature element of the Victorian, Arts and Crafts, Country, and Neoclassical styles. Directions for a Victorian wainscot project using bead-board panels begin on page 57; a Cottage Country wall paneling project, also using bead-board panels, is on page 84. Here are general guidelines and construction options.

Traditional wainscoting is made up of bead board—milled wood boards measuring about ⅜ inch thick by about 4 inches wide. Bead board has a tongue on one side and a groove on the other, features that create invisible joints and a seamless installation. Plywood panels with embossed beading are also available; their surface isn't as richly detailed as true bead board, but the large pieces make installation quick. Preprimed wainscot panel kits are also available in limited styles.

Some wainscot, particularly in the Arts and Crafts style, is made up of a flat panel, often richly grained, trimmed with battens. If you plan to paint the wainscot, it can be made of plain plywood, with or without battens (see photo 5, page 122).

The general rule in a wainscoting project is to cover either one third or two thirds of the wall; common wainscot heights are thus 32 to 36 inches, or about 60 inches. Avoid a height that cuts the wall in half horizontally, which will not be nearly as pleasing. Cap your wainscoting with simple, flat moldings, a chair rail, or a plate shelf and brackets.

1 Bead board capped with simple, flat stock creates a classic Country or Arts and Crafts look. Topped with a more elaborate molding, it sheds its casual appeal for a more formal image. To install bead board, glue it to the wall and drive 18-gauge brads or 4d nails through the board tongue, countersinking the fasteners enough that the groove of the adjoining board can slide over the tongue. Note: Glue is essential when installing over wallboard; you rarely hit a framing member, and the boards might otherwise come loose. The chair rail, if any, can be returned onto the casing (page 111), but avoid doing this with baseboard or wainscoting.

Wainscoting techniques continue >

Tip

To move the wainscot profile out, or to deal with an uneven wall surface, install 1 × 4 furring strips—horizontal boards that support the wainscoting—at the top, middle, and bottom of the wall, nailing them into the framing. Then nail the bead board to the furring strips. Note, however, that moving the wainscoting out requires casings deep enough that the wainscoting and baseboard can die into them.

2 Beaded plywood paneling can substitute for bead board, imparting much the same look. It's quick and easy to put a whole room together with these panels. Install them as shown here: Fasten the panels with nails and glue, then glue and nail a top molding in place.

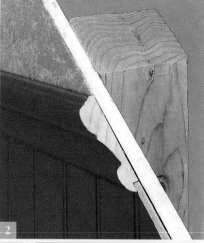

3 You can create wainscot wall panels with plywood bridged by 1 × 3s, 1 × 4s, or other flat stock. Fill in the panels with matching or contrasting paint or wallpaper.

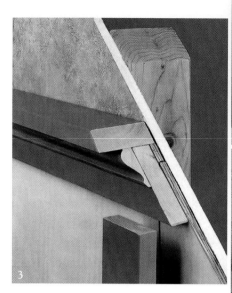

4 Adding mitered cap molding further defines the panels and creates a much more formal effect.

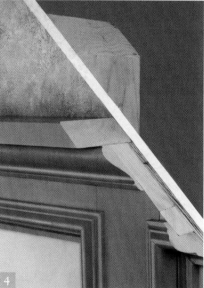

5 Wainscot with battens can be "painted out"—painted the same color as the surrounding walls and trim. The monochromatic scheme plays down the trim, so it is more texture than pattern. In white, it's particularly suitable to a Cottage Country style.

working with composite moldings

Modern composite moldings can be an attractive alternative to wood. Available in a variety of synthetic compositions, they offer the richness and depth of plaster or carved hardwood at a more economical price. They're also a good substitute for multipart, built-up moldings that require several separate pieces of wood. In the two examples shown here, note the corner pieces. Such pieces eliminate the need to miter or cope corners. The lower example shows an easy way to create ornate wall panels.

If you want a more elaborate look than typical softwood moldings provide, consider these products. Their advantages include light weight, which is a boon if you're working alone. Flexible polymer moldings can be bent around curved walls. Shrinkage for all composites is much less than that for wood, and composites are impervious to water and insects. Composites are usually supplied pre-primed, ready for painting or faux finishing. (A natural wood finish isn't possible.) Sanding is not necessary.

You can install composites just as you would ordinary wood moldings, as described in the preceding pages. Composites can be cut, drilled, nailed, glued, and screwed just like wood. Some manufacturers recommend you use a hand miter box for cutting. If you use a power miter saw, be sure to use a fine-tooth blade with little set to the teeth. This will help prevent tearing.

You can nail the moldings in place, but the best practice is to fasten high-density polyurethane and similar products with trim-head wallboard screws. These are self-countersinking, leaving a hole that you fill with wall patching compound. Predrilling is usually not necessary. Alternatively, you can install composite moldings with nails and a siliconized latex caulking used as an adhesive/bedding compound/gap filler. Wood adhesives can also be used.

finishing

When possible, finish the trim before installing it. This saves a lot of fussy work later. The inevitable dings and nicks in the finished pieces are easy to touch up after they're put in place. Whether you do your finishing before installation or after, proper preparation is the key.

If you plan to stain the trim, avoid exposed end grain in your trim work. It's difficult to keep the end grain from absorbing a lot of color, which looks unattractive. It will look better if you cut and fit returns instead (page 111).

1 After the wall patching compound or wood putty has dried (page 108), sand carefully with 120-grit paper. Start by leveling the filled areas, then sand the entire surface. You can use a damp rag or tack cloth to wipe off the sanding dust.

2 For a painted surface, before or after priming but before the final painting, fill all gaps with painter's caulk. For a stained and clear-finished surface, apply clear or tinted silicone-based caulk after staining and clear finishing.

PAINTED FINISHES

After sanding, apply a coat of primer and sand again lightly with 150-grit paper to knock down any raised grain.

Over the sanded primer, apply two coats of final finish, sanding with 220-grit paper between coats. You can use either alkyd (solvent-based) or acrylic (water-based) enamels for interior trim. Although solvent-based paints were previously preferred for looks and durability, modern acrylics are now widely embraced by professional painters for their ease of application and cleanup, and for their environmental friendliness and greater health safety.

Painted trim is almost always finished in satin or gloss enamel (page 23). The extra reflectance imparts a glow to the moldings, helping them to stand out from flat-finished or wallpapered walls and enhancing their appearance. It also provides a more durable, washable surface. In general, the glossier the paint the more durable it is.

CLEAR FINISHES

For clear-finished moldings, sand smooth; if you're staining the trim, apply one or more coats. If you're using water-based stain, you may need to sand, with 220-grit paper, before finishing to knock down any grain raised by the water. Top-coat with a clear finish for protection.

TOOLS AND METHODS

A good finish job requires good brushes. For small moldings, a 1½-inch angled sash brush is ideal; a 2-inch square-cut trim brush is best for wider work. Start at the top with the high, horizontal surfaces, such as crown molding, mantel shelf, or column capitals. Then do the casings (head casings first, then the sides), columns, pilasters, and wainscoting. Base-board comes last. Whether you're painting or clear-coating, apply the finish to the top and bottom edges of trim pieces first, then fill in the center sections, maintaining a wet edge as you go.

glossary

back band: trim that wraps over top of paneling or flat casing

baseboard: trim that covers base of wall and junction with floor

base cap: molded trim that sits on top of baseboard

base shoe molding: trim that covers the bottom of baseboard, shaped like an elongated quarter-round

batten: narrow strip of wood

beaded molding: molding with one or more rounded strips running lengthwise

bed molding: molding that combines quarter-round and cove detail

bevel: on the edge of a board, a lengthwise cut that is not 90 degrees

brick molding: trim traditionally used on house exterior to cover joint between brick and wood siding, with a curve to direct water away from siding

cap molding: trim that wraps over the top of paneling or flat casing

carved molding: molding with a decorative profile carved by machine or hand, such as a corbel or wood onlay

casing: trim around windows and doors

ceiling or cornice molding: covers the top of a wall and junction with ceiling, or tops an entablature

chair rail: a horizontal wall trim applied approximately 36 inches from the floor

chamfer: a beveled edge, usually at a 45-degree angle

clamshell molding: plain casing with a slightly curved front

corbel: plain or carved block that projects from a wall to support weight, such as a beam

corner molding: an L-shaped trim

cove molding: concave molding used to cover joint between moldings

crown molding: cornice molding that crosses the intersection of wall and ceiling at an angle

dado: decorated lower part of a wall, usually the bottom 36 inches

dentil molding: trim composed of small blocks at regular intervals, slightly resembling a row of teeth

die into: said of a piece of trim when it butts into a thicker trim at right angles

doorstop molding: a narrow molding used on a jamb to halt the door's movement

egg-and-dart molding: trim composed of alternating ovals and arrowheads

entablature: the top of a door or window surround, made up of casing, frieze, and cornice

finger joint: a method of joining two boards end to end with interlocking notches

fluted molding: trim with shallow vertical grooves cut along its face in parallel lines

frieze: a horizontal panel of a surround, often ornamented

half-round: a molding with a semicircular profile

head cap: trim that tops the casing above a window or door

lintel: a beam or board support across the top of a door, window, or fireplace

mantel, mantel shelf: projecting horizontal board above a fireplace

molded trim: milled trim with a decorative profile

ogee: molding with an S-shaped profile

on center: method of measuring from the center point of one element—usually a stud—to the center of the next

overmantel: the area above a fireplace frame or mantel

panel molding: molding that is used to create wall frames or panels

picture molding/rail: horizontal trim, run along the upper portion of a wall, with a rounded edge from which picture hooks can hang

pilaster: a flat rectangular column set against a wall or to frame a door, window, or fireplace

plinth block: a piece that forms the projecting base of casing or a column

profile: contour of the face of a molding, visible in cross section

quarter-round: a molding with a profile that is a quarter of a circle

rabbet: a straight-edged cut in the end or edge of a board, usually made to accommodate a joining piece

reeded molding: trim with lengths of parallel narrow convex strips divided by grooves

rip: to cut along the grain of a piece of lumber

shingle molding: ogee-shaped trim traditionally used in Victorian homes to cap end of roof sheathing

square-cut: to cut across the grain, at exactly 90 degrees, and perfectly straight

stamped molding: molding in which the profile has been stamped into its face rather than molded or carved

step casing: a casing with three graduated steps of thickness

suite of trim: a grouping of trim—such as baseboard, casings, and cornice—coordinated to work together within a room

toenail: method of attaching the end of one board to the face of another by nailing at an angle, used when it's not possible to drive a nail straight through one into the other

wainscot: wood paneling on part of a wall, generally the lower one third or two thirds

wall frame: a rectilinear shape made of thin molding and affixed to a wall to resemble a wall panel

wall panel: a raised or recessed section of wall decoration

wrap, wrap onto: to go around the edge of

interior trim resources

Local lumberyards, millwork suppliers, and home improvement centers usually carry many of the trim materials specified for the projects in this book. For a broader selection and for specialty items, you may have to order from a catalog or the Internet. Following are some companies that may be able to supply materials you need. Any company that is "to the trade only" can be contacted through an architect or interior designer.

MOLDING AND DECORATIVE TRIM SUPPLIERS

Balmer Architectural Mouldings
271 Yorkland Blvd.
Toronto, Ontario
M2J1S5 Canada
416-491-6425
www.balmer.com

Polyurethane trim; mantels; ceiling domes, rosettes, and medallions; wall niches. Request a sample kit of moldings

Chadsworth, Inc.
277 North Front St.
Historic Wilmington, NC 28401
800-columns (265-8667)
www.columns.com

Wood columns

Classic Details
P.O. Box 280144
Columbia, SC 29228
803-356-4545
www.classicdetails.com

Wood and polyurethane moldings, ceiling medallions and rosettes, brackets, corbels, embossed onlays

Cumberland Woodcraft Co.
P.O. Drawer 609
Carlisle, PA 17013
800-367-1884
www.cumberlandwoodcraft.com

Wood moldings, corbels, brackets, ornaments, Victorian trim

Decorative Concepts
Boise, Idaho
(866) 328-8033
www.decorativeconcepts.net

Wood fireplace surrounds and mantel shelves

Outwater Plastics Industries
4 Passaic St.
P.O. Drawer 403
Woodridge, NJ 07075
800-631-8375
www.outwater.com

Polyurethane and wood trim, wall and ceiling panels, sculpted ceiling tiles, columns, pilasters, pediments, ceiling beams, fireplace surrounds

Raymond Enkeboll Designs
16506 Avalon Blvd.
Carson, CA 90706
800-745-5507
www.enkeboll.com

Fine carved trim, architectural moldings, fireplaces (to the trade only)

The Mantel Shop
730 W. Paseo Verde, Unit A
Nogales, AZ 85621
888-367-5771
www.mantelshop.com

Wood mantel shelves and fireplace surrounds

Vintage Woodworks
Hwy. 34S
P.O. Box 39
Quinlan, TX 75474-0039
903-356-2158
www.vintagewoodworks.com

Vintage and Victorian wood moldings, corner block and corner post trim systems, bead board, cornices, spandrels, corbels, mantel shelves, pilasters

ZaGo Manufacturing Company, Inc.
190 Murray Street
Newark, NJ 07114
973-643-6700
www.flexibletrims.com

Flexible polymer trim

SHOJI PANELS

Pinecrest, Inc.
2118 Blaisdell Ave.
Minneapolis, MN 55404
612-871-7071
www.pinecrestinc.com

Shoji panels

Shoji Designs
P.O. Box 1122
Olalla, WA 98359
253-857-4712
www.shojidesigns.com

Custom shoji panels and track systems

credits

PHOTOGRAPHY

Courtesy of Cherry Tree Design: 92-93; Gary Conaughton: 73, 75; Scott Fitzgerrell: 1 center, center right, and bottom, 3 center right and bottom, 13 bottom, 94, 96-107, 108 top, 109-110, 111 center and bottom, 112-123, 124 top; Tria Giovan: 10 top, 14 bottom, 20 left, 39 top, 81 left; Ken Gutmaker: 91; Jamie Hadley: 2 left, 51, 63 bottom, 68, 77, 84, 87; John M. Hall: 2 top right, 40; Philip Harvey: 49, 50; Dennis Krukowski: 4 bottom, 17 bottom, 39 bottom, 44, 59; David Duncan Livingston: 24 bottom, 53, 81 top right; Sylvia Martin: 1 center left, 69, 86 bottom; E. Andrew McKinney: 3 center left, 24 top right, 63 top, 65; Emily Minton: 46;

Robert Perron: 3 top, 4 center left, 10 bottom left and right, 11, 15, 20 right, 24 center right, 62, 78, 85 left and right; Kenneth Rice: 82 top; George Ross: 24 center left, 54; Mark Samu: 19, 21 top, 31, 45, 74, 76; Michael Skott: 4 top right, 7 top, 21 bottom, 22, 80 bottom, 83 right; Tim Street-Porter/Beateworks.com: 4 center right, 8, 64; Brian Vanden Brink: 1 top left and right, 2 bottom right, 4 top left, 6, 12, 14 top right, 18, 24 top left and center, 28, 32, 35, 38, 42, 47, 52, 57, 61, 71 top and bottom right, 81 bottom right, 82-83 bottom, 83 top, 86 top, 88; Christopher Vendetta: 108 bottom, 111 top, 124 bottom; David Wakely: 70; Jessie Walker: 4 center, 5, 7 bottom, 9, 13, 14 top and center left, center right, 16, 17 top, 23, 25, 26, 27, 30, 37, 56, 71 left, 79, 80 top, 90; Karen Witynski: 89.

DESIGNERS

Kendall Agins, design: 77; **John Allison, AIA, Allison Architects:** 46; **David Andreozzi,** design: 3 top, 24 center right, 78; **Julie Atwood,** design: 63 bottom, 68; **James Beyor,** architect: 4 top left, 6; **Samuel Botero & Associates,** design: 4 bottom; **Mona Branagh, Pacific Interiors:** 50; **Brenco Designs:** 70; **Bullock & Co. Log Home Builders:** 83 top; **Sherrill Canet Design:** 19; **Centerbrook,** architects: 71 bottom; **Cherry Tree Design:** 92–93; **Cornerstone Builders:** 79; **Stephen Foote,** architect: 24 top left, 28; **Mark Hampton, Inc.:** 44; **Stephen Harby,** design: 4 center right, 8, 64; **Dan Hasselgrave, Structura,** design: 85; **Hearst Specials:** 31, 74; **Jarvis Architects:** 87; **Ken Kelly,** design: 45; **Carol Knott, ASID:** 14 top left, 17 top; **Adele Lampert, ASID:** 16 bottom; **Llemeau et cie:** 39 bottom, 59; **Kate Marchesini, Acorn Design Interiors:** 24 center left, 54; **McMillen, Inc.,** design: 17 bottom; **Carolyn Miller,** design: 76; **John Morris,** architect: 61; **Robert Orr,** design: 62; **Kit Parmentier/Allison Rose,** design: 2 left, 84; **Alejandro Patrón,** design: 89; **Peterson.Arce Design Group:** 73, 75; **Remick Associates:** 49; **Mark Shure,** design: 91; **Simonson & Baric,** painting: 4 bottom; **Winton Scott,** architect: 14 top right, 18; **Sam Schofield,** architect: 21 top; **Jack Silverio,** architect: 71 top; **South Mountain Builders:** 82–83 bottom; **Charles Spada:** 4 center left, 11; **Stephanie Stokes:** 2 top right, 40; **Dennis Welch-May,** design: 15, 20 right; **Jack Weyna, ASID:** 56; **Katie White, ASID:** 14 center left, 23.

ACKNOWLEDGEMENTS

We would like to thank the homeowners who allowed us to photograph in their homes. Thanks also to Mount Storm Forest Products, Windsor, Calif., and Don White of White Brothers Architectural Moldings and Mill, Oakland, Calif., for their assistance.

index